S0-BSH-391

THE PROCESS
OF SCHOOLING

A Psychological
Examination

J. M. STEPHENS
The University of British Columbia

HOLT, RINEHART AND WINSTON, INC.

NEW YORK   CHICAGO   SAN FRANCISCO   ATLANTA
DALLAS   TORON'

LB
1051
.S74

Copyright © 1967 by Holt, Rinehart and Winston, Inc.

All rights reserved

Library of Congress Catalog Card Number: 67-19442

2560605

Printed in the United States of America

1 2 3 4 5 6 7 8 9

PREFACE

The theory of spontaneous schooling was brought to testable form just after World War II and one must go back almost another twenty years to find its inception. During the late 1920s I began to suspect that there must be some powerful forces to be found within the child's social environment (the forces of schooling) that would dependably invoke the internal mechanisms by which children were able to learn. The existence of such powerful forces in the child's social environment seemed not only an advantage but actually a grim survival necessity.

In searching for valid forces of schooling, it was natural to give much thought to the mechanisms of learning through which such forces would have to work. In 1928 or 1929 the most logical principle of learning seemed to be the "law of effect" as propounded by Thorndike, and it was on this principle that I began to build. About the very time that I began to erect my structure on this principle, however, developments were already in motion which, for a time, seemed about to demolish the law of effect itself. Pavlov had just been translated into English, and the "conditioned response" appealed to many people as an attractive mechanistic substitute for the law of effect with its alleged mentalistic taint. Hull had just moved to Yale and was about to extol the superior explanatory virtues of this Pavlovian notion. To crown the irony, Thorndike himself, in the early 1930s, disavowed that portion of the law of effect which involved punishment. He now claimed that it did no good to say "no" when a pupil made a mistake. It was on the influence of this form of punishment, moreover, that I had relied most heavily in framing the spontaneous forces of schooling.

In the face of this disaster I brashly set out, almost single-handedly as I supposed, to restore the law of effect and to restore it in its unmutilated form. In a series of investigations that were to continue until World War II, I tried to show (1) that the law of effect could be regarded as quite mechanistic, (2) that the rival conditioned response could not function as an explanation of learning unless it covertly invoked the law of effect, (3) that the law of effect had explanatory powers not available to the conditioned response, and (4) that in spite of Thorndike's apostasy, punishment did contribute to the learning process.

Long before this crusade had ended, there was ample evidence that I was not so much alone as I had thought. On the basis of their own activities, many theorists were coming to give more and more serious consideration to the law of effect, now re-christened "reinforcement theory" to fit in with Pavlovian language. With the dramatic about-face of Hull in 1936, one of the outstanding critics of the law of effect now became its chief standard bearer. By this time there was every justification for invoking reinforcement or effect as a serious principle of learning.

For a time, I am afraid, I secretly resented the fact that better men than I had so developed the psychology of learning that my own efforts were unnecessary and rather insignificant. Since these others had legitimized the principle that I really needed, I might well have retired from the controversy regarding learning theory and have turned my attention exclusively to the refinement of the theory of schooling. I had by now become interested in the controversy for its own sake, however, and continued to give it much of my attention until interrupted by the war.

The intensive study of learning had clearly made it possible to invoke the principle of reinforcement. Ironically enough, moreover, this same study had also freed the theory of schooling from complete dependence on the principle of reinforcement. The furious controversy in the field of learning had by no means achieved a consensus. But it did succeed in producing a clear-cut picture of the similarities and differences between the rival theories. It was this picture that Hilgard was able to document and describe so admirably in his classic 1948 statement. With this increasing clarification of the alternatives, I was able to show, to my own satisfaction at least, that the spontaneous forces held to be responsible for schooling could operate through any or all of the rival principles of learning likely to be proposed (see Chapter 6).

At this point, the theory of spontaneous schooling was largely roughed out. I was now to spend the next twenty years trying to achieve a satisfactory test of the theory, and trying to bring it to the attention of scholars in the field. To one of my impractical bent, these two tasks proved much more formidable than the intrinsic task of developing the theory. Apart from a pilot study generously supported by the Canadian Defence Research Medical Laboratories, I was almost completely unsuccessful in securing a test. For many years, moreover, attempts to publish a unified account also met with complete failure. Publication of selected segments, however, became possible through the generosity of the editors of *School and Society, Educational Theory, The Journal of Educational Psychology, The School Review,* and *Theory Into Practice.* I had become convinced that such piecemeal publication would have to suffice when, to my surprise, David Boynton of Holt, Rinehart and Winston asked to see the complete account.

I must mention my gratitude to scores of students and colleagues who encouraged me, put up with me, and corrected me. I also look back with appreciation to the half-a-lifetime at The Johns Hopkins University and to the unusual opportunity for sustained and irresponsible thought.

I wish to express my gratitude to Marilyn Henshaw and to my wife for their unusual skill and patience in making sense out of the vague assortment of mumblings and jottings with which they had to deal.

Vancouver, Canada   J. M. S.
April 1967

CONTENTS

PART ONE

INTRODUCTION

1 | THE ARGUMENT IN BRIEF

The current and growing agitation about education and the schools has expressed itself in a demand for immediate reform and for an increase in efficiency. We are urged to provide more lavish support, to reform the course of study, to extend the training of teachers, and to make that training more realistic. Whenever we seek additional information, our searches are chiefly directed to such pressing practical problems as mental retardation and effective programs for the gifted, and to the possible advantages from educational television, from programmed instruction and from other technical innovations.

If we are to carry out these improvements in any effective fashion, we should have some understanding of the process we seek to modify. To operate on the gigantic scale now being considered, we ought to have an understanding that is very precise indeed. We ought to know the forces that bring schools and schooling into existence. We also ought to know, in some detail, the forces and mechanisms that lead the schools to continue to accomplish that which they have in the past.

As yet, unfortunately, we can make no claim to any coherent group of principles from which the major facts of schooling and teaching could be deduced. Such, at least, is the universal lament of those who approach the subject (Coladarci, 1958; Gage, 1963, pp. 132–133; Wiseman, 1959).

It is true, of course, that we do have thousands of investigations regarding the effectiveness of this or that specific device. Regarding the essential underlying mechanisms of schooling, however, we even lack serious detailed speculation, to say nothing of convincing evidence.

Although we lack any clearly acceptable theory of schooling, we might be able, it is true, to detect an implicit theory underlying the various proposals that are made. Insofar as we can detect such a theory, we must conclude that it places great stress on the formal curriculum, on the program of instruction, and on the administrative features of education. Certainly, these are the forces we seek to manipulate when we direct our efforts toward the improvement of education.

This preoccupation with the conspicuous and artificial aspects of education reminds one of an amusing, if spurious, account of the origins of agriculture. There was once a suggestion that, in some early burial services, it was customary to place wild grain in the grave for the use of the deceased in his new life. Inevitably some of this grain was spilled around the edge of the grave. In that fertile soil it took root and flourished, ultimately providing a harvest. The survivors noticed this result, and soon a definite principle was formulated: At a certain season, bury a corpse with all the proper ceremonies, and in due course there will be grain to harvest. The corpse, of course, was the most prominent feature of the process, and it became the focal point around which the whole principle was organized. When the planting season came around, corpses were in great demand and were even produced to order when not otherwise available. It was upon the treatment of the corpse, moreover, that the success of the harvest was supposed to depend. It was not until many years later that some bold radical questioned the value of this main feature of the process and found, after experimentation, that the planting would be almost as effective if there were no corpse at all.

It is easy to focus our attention on the conspicuous, dramatic events that call for deliberate decisions. Conversely, it is natural to ignore the humble, ever-present forces that work consistently, independent of our concern. Seeds sprout and take root, and plants mature, with little attention from us. Corpses, on the other hand, call for deliberate and careful attention.

There is a disturbing possibility that the elaborate program of instruction in our educational system may be somewhat similar to the corpse in the planting ceremonies. Like the corpse, it is the most conspicuous feature of the process. Like the corpse, this program of instruction absorbs most of our attention. Just as our predecessors tried to improve the agricultural process by elaborate alterations in the management of the corpse, so we try to improve the educational process by elaborate and refined changes in the program of instruction. But, as with the corpse, this program of instruction may turn out to be a mere incidental feature in the educational process. The essential features of education may reside not in the program itself but in a few primitive forces which always accompany the program. These processes, like those involved in the germination of seeds, are so humble and so automatic that they demand little attention. Yet, they may provide the basic mechanisms on which all educational activities depend. Such, at least, is the contention of this book.

It is time we took a serious look at these lowly forces. So great is our need for an understanding of the basic forces in schooling, indeed, that, for a time, we could properly divert some of our effort from the urgent practical problems that beset us, and direct it toward a reasonable understanding of the schooling process itself. In thus casting our bread upon the waters of disinterested inquiry, we stand a reasonable chance of attaining practical gains out of all proportion to the effort expended.

It is not only on practical grounds that such a disinterested study of education is demanded (Stephens, 1933). Unless we are to disown the human urge to comprehend, we are bound to try to understand this complex, but all too familiar, process of schooling. We cannot face these ever-recurring phenomena of schooling without asking, "Why? What are the basic processes that underlie these events?"

It is toward such an understanding that this book is directed. In a very general way, we are concerned with the underlying forces responsible for the very existence of schools, and, in a more intensive way, we are concerned with the forces underlying the work that the schools accomplish. Suppose, as an exaggerated illustration, we had to design a new species. Suppose further that we wanted these new creatures to develop schools that would resemble those that we now know as well as schools that would accomplish something of what our current schools accomplish. What kind of forces or mechanisms should we install in our new creatures to guarantee these results?

We can look at the current schools from much the same point of view. We could seek to determine the historical forces which led to the emergence of schools. We could ask about the pressures which led the schools to concentrate on some areas of the child's development and to give less attention to other areas. We could also ask about the forces responsible for the work that schools of all eras have accomplished. Even more pointedly we can ask why it is that the outcomes of schooling respond so grudgingly to deliberate efforts at acceleration.

It is to the accomplishment of the current school and to the constancy of that accomplishment that this inquiry is directed. Prior to beginning this more business-like analysis, however, it may help to look at the broader picture and to consider the kind of forces that may have been at work to bring schools and schooling into existence.

In this highly speculative account of the possible origin of the schools, there will be little stress on the deliberate, rational decisions so frequently invoked to account for human activities. Contrariwise, our account puts its faith in primitive, spontaneous tendencies that have developed as the race evolved. It is contended that these blind, unknowing tendencies probably antedated rational decisions, and that they would have led to the establishment of schools or near-schools even in the absence of deliberate, rational intent.

To obtain the most satisfactory understanding of the origin of the schools, we should see these primitive tendencies in the light of their alleged survival function. Our account maintains that these tendencies responsible for the origin of the schools supplement other spontaneous tendencies such as those involved in primitive child care. The school-producing tendencies allegedly combined with the more primitive tendencies in such a way as to favor the survival of those groups fortunate enough to possess the tendencies and to give them expression.

In this general notion of the origin of the schools, survival is the key. To have a good chance of survival, members of a group must attain reasonable proficiency in many different kinds of behavior. Typically, these ways of behaving, or tendencies, call for nurture or cultivation. It follows, then, that a group is more likely to survive if it has mechanisms for the necessary cultivation of these useful tendencies.

Some essential tendencies, such as breathing or swallowing, have immediate survival value. These tendencies are developed by practically foolproof mechanisms in which nurture plays little part. Other tendencies, such as those involved in the eating of reasonably nutritious foods, are also important to survival, but they permit some latitude and can be developed by a more haphazard system. Typically, they are nurtured by parents and by the built-in concerns to which parents give automatic expression. Finally, there are scores of frivolous, playful, or decorative tendencies which for years contribute nothing immediately to survival but which, on rare occasions, have made tremendous contributions to the survival of the group. For instance, the tendency to make marks on rocks probably had little or no direct influence on the survival of the group. As part of the basis for written communication, however, these tendencies would ultimately make an enormous contribution to survival.

These playful, decorative tendencies typically lead to behavior for which parents feel little immediate and urgent concern, although they feel some remote, yet indulgent, interest. The three-year-old's failure to engage in oral conversation would constitute a daily and disturbing worry. His failure to read or write, on the other hand, would be a matter of more remote concern. Parents would be less forcibly and less frequently reminded of the deficiency. Their reaction to the deficiency, moreover, would be less drastic and less positive. Very often such a reaction would prompt a resolution to look into the matter one of these days. Nevertheless, in the long run, the average parent feels some remote and indulgent concern for his child's ability to read. When, upon occasion, he becomes aware of competence in this area, he is pleased. When some infrequent event occurs to remind him of a deficiency, he is disturbed. This remote, sporadic, and indulgent concern is far different from that shown for a deficiency in eating, walking, talking, or in the ordinary social graces.

For any culture there is bound to be such behavior as reading, singing, and ceremonial knot tying as well as knowledge of the tribal legends for which the typical home feels some patronizing and moderate concern, although the concern is insufficient to guarantee the nurture necessary for competence in this area. These areas vary from culture to culture and from one period to another.

Some unpredictable few of these many "useless," playful, or decorative tendencies may turn out, generations later, to have enormous survival value. It follows, therefore, that the society which has evolved some means of nurturing these luxury traits would, in the long run, have an advantage over any society which limited its nurture to those traits having an immediate and obvious payoff. It is held that in most surviving societies something similar to a school or near-school has evolved. Such schools, or the near-schools of the extended family, have given the same immediate, daily, and urgent concern to reading, learning history, or dancing as the more immediate home typically provides for talking or for the proper handling of sharp instruments.

This unique function or curriculum of the traditional school, or quasi-school, in any culture, could be described in two ways. First, this curriculum is a helter-skelter sample drawn from the playful and decorative tendencies. These tendencies, it will be remembered, have little or no immediate survival value. Some unpredictable few, however, may have an enormous survival value for the future, provided they receive adequate cultivation. Second, the school curriculum includes some of the traits, but not necessarily all, for which the parents in the culture feel a general permissive, supportive interest, although they express little daily, urgent, and continuing concern.

Although the schools in various cultures have actually performed a survival role, it is not to be supposed that the people in the schools have typically been conscious of this survival function; nor should they be. Many activities will work more smoothly and dependably in promoting survival when the people involved give little or no thought to the ultimate survival significance of their behavior. Biological procreation, to use an analogy, would be intolerably precarious if it depended upon behavior deliberately undertaken for the sake of procreation. Survival is most likely to be assured by procreative activities which appeal to the participants as attractive in their own right but which also have important survival by-products. Similarly, any survival value that may reside in literature, incantations, or ritualistic sand painting is much more likely to be promoted if the teacher cherishes these activities as important ends in themselves. He would cultivate them in less dedicated fashion if he viewed them primarily as weird activities having a possible but highly problematic survival value for some remote future.

In such speculation, the very existence of schooling may stem not from a deliberate decision of groups or societies but from blind, spontaneous tendencies which are developed by evolutionary demand and which are found to be prevalent in human beings, although more pronounced in some people than in others.

There are two categories of these blind, automatic forces that may have played a crucial part in the gradual evolution of schooling. One category contains the playful, manipulative tendencies already stressed. These are the tendencies, devoid of immediate utility, that lead us to make marks in the sand, to drop rocks into pools, to play with echoes, or to hit balls with sticks. In another category we find extremely powerful but unpremeditated tendencies to communicate. In spontaneous, unthinking fashion we find ourselves telling others of our interests or experiences. Quite spontaneously we react to the way others behave in matters that interest us. Our reaction may consist of spontaneous applause or an ill-concealed shudder; we may be compelled to correct someone or to supply the solution or the word for which someone else is groping.

The tendencies responsible for behavior that has little immediate survival value are widespread and powerful. So are the primitive tendencies to communicate. The tendencies in both categories often function without the aid of elaborate rational decisions. Indeed, they often function when rational decisions say, "No."

These tendencies, which are present in all individuals, are especially strong in some of us. People thus endowed are likely to find children the most convenient audience for their communications. From the combination of these forces and circumstances, schools of some kind are almost bound to result, whether or not the community or the people involved have given any thought to the desirability of such institutions.

Whatever the grim facts of prehistory, we have claimed that these spontaneous forces, given moderately free rein, have led to the establishment of schools, and have directed those schools to the task of developing traits which have remote and problematic survival value. We now turn to the central problem, and inquire about the basic mechanisms by which the school accomplishes the mission that it has thus acquired. At this point, the psychologist must turn to his own domain. He is no longer able to excuse himself from seeking out hard data that bear on his theories.

How does the school induce learning in its pupils? To influence pupils, the school must have at its disposal certain forces or mechanisms that are capable of engaging the mechanisms of learning which may be found within the child. Not surprisingly, the same spontaneous tendencies, blithely proposed to account for the existence of the schools, can now, in very serious fashion, be invoked as the mechanisms responsible for the day-by-day work of the schools. The spontaneous tendencies which gave rise to the schools in the first place are the same tendencies, now operating in the service of the schools, that engage those mechanisms of learning which are to be found within the pupil. This linkage is not surprising. It is easy to speculate that the spontaneous tendencies and the mechanisms of learning probably evolved hand in hand.

Whatever they may have done for the genesis of the schools, the postulated spontaneous tendencies are bound to engage the mechanisms of learning. An adult with a strong interest in, say, algebra, and with a liberal supply of the communicative tendencies will automatically induce children to respond to some of the notions in algebra. He will also reinforce or accept proper responses, will correct erroneous responses, will point the way to the right answers, and will sharpen the pupil's insight into the relations between procedures and outcomes. In these events we find a composite list of the mechanisms of learning stressed in one theory or another. Because of his spontaneous tendencies, the adult effectively engages those mechanisms of learning and does so whether or not his intention is to teach.

One of the psychological phenomena to be explained is the remarkable constancy of educational results in the face of widely differing deliberate approaches. Every so often we adopt new approaches or new methodologies and place our reliance on new panaceas. At the very least we seem to chorus new slogans. Yet the academic growth within the classroom continues at about the same rate, stubbornly refusing to cooperate with the bright new dicta emanating from the conference room.

This constancy of academic growth is treated at length in Chapter 7. Meanwhile we merely may note that it is an ancient and persisting phenomenon. It is also a phenomenon that is readily explained by the postulated residual concerns, coupled with the spontaneous communicative tendencies that are also invoked by the theory.

The constancy of the school's accomplishment is one of those things that everybody knows. It is part of the folklore that, in educational investigations, one method turns out to be as good as another and that promising innovations produce about as much growth as the procedures they supplant, but no more. Nachman and Opochinsky (1958), to take one example, feel safe in stating, as a matter of common knowledge, that "Reviews of teaching research have consistently concluded that different teaching procedures produce little or no difference in the amount of knowledge gained by the students." In truth this has been a refrain ever since Rice (1897) discovered the surprising constancy of spelling attainment in the face of marked variations in the time devoted to study and since Merriam (1915) reported regular growth in school subjects in the absence of formal instruction in those subjects.

These classical conclusions are echoed when we turn to the most recent studies of television and programmed instruction. After reviewing some 393 separate investigations comparing television with other forms of instruction, Schramm (1962) found that 255 of these investigations reported no significant difference, and of the 138 reporting significant differences, 83 showed a superiority for TV, and 55 reported superior results from the traditional classroom. Comparisons of programmed instruction with regular forms of study again reveal no clear-cut advantage or disadvantage for either procedure (Feldhusen, 1963; Poppleton and Austwick, 1964). True enough, however, like other forms of individualized instruction, programmed instruction permits a saving of time for some students.

Team teaching gets good results, but the results are not consistently better than those gained from traditional teaching (Ginther and Shrayer, 1962). The appropriate claim for team teaching is to say that it is at least as good as the traditional procedures (White, 1964).

Bracketed between the ancient and the most recent investigations are scores of studies to show that pupils learn about as much in large classes as in small classes (De Cecco, 1964; Fleming, 1959); in homogeneous groups as in heterogeneous groups (Ekstrom, 1961); in core curricula as in traditional curricula (Michelson, 1957); in lecture classes as in discussion classes (Churchill and John, 1958; McKeachie, 1963); in teacher-centered approaches as in group-centered approaches (Stern, 1963); in small schools with indifferent facilities as in large schools with lavish facilities (Lathrop, 1960).

The relative constancy in the achievements of the schools, as roughly sketched above, should be no surprise to anyone who believed in the theory of spontaneous schooling. According to this theory, the mechanisms actually responsible for academic growth reside in humble, spontaneous tendencies which are always in operation when an adult consorts with maturing children. True enough, such tendencies should be freer to operate in some circumstances than in others. But the conditions essential for effective operation would not necessarily reflect the differences in administrative arrangements. Many of these primitive forces might function just as well in large classes as in small, with one formal method as with another, in a primitive one-room school as in the latest architectural triumph.

The theory, as sketched, is intended solely to make sense out of what we see in the phenomena of schooling. As a disinterested theory, it is not directly concerned with suggesting improvements in practice. It is content with explaining some familiar phenomena and subjecting them to a measure of order.

Still any theory, however disinterested, may have some practical implications, and this is certainly true of the present theory. Such implications, derived as they are from an untested theory, should be regarded not so much as prescriptions for reform but as elaborations of some features of the theory that could not so readily be exposed in any other way. According to the pragmatic notion, it is from the practical implications of a theory that its inner nature can best be known.

If this theory should be true, we would be making a great mistake in regarding the management of schools as similar to the process of constructing a building or operating a factory. In these latter processes, deliberate decisions play a crucial part, and the enterprise advances or stands still in proportion to the amount of deliberate effort exerted. If we must use a metaphor or model in seeking to understand the process of schooling, we should look to agriculture rather than to the factory. In agriculture we do not start from scratch, and we do not direct our efforts to inert and passive materials. We start, on the contrary, with a complex and ancient process, and we organize our efforts around what seeds, plants, and insects are likely to do anyway. Through an improved understanding of these organic processes we can almost revolutionize the output, but we do not supplant or ignore these older organic forces. We always work through them.

Such a metaphor, such a view, would invite a somewhat relaxed attitude toward education once the basic forces are set in motion. The crop, once planted, may undergo some development even while the farmer sleeps or loafs. No matter what he does, *some* aspects of the outcome will remain constant. When teachers and pupils foregather, some education may proceed even while the Superintendent disports himself in Atlantic City.

Our relaxed attitude would extend to the recruitment and treatment of teachers. According to this theory, teachers need not be the paragons of virtue and skill so often suggested in inspirational commencement addresses. In filling the thousands of classroom positions, we need no longer restrict ourselves to these model creatures. Whenever they are in short supply, we can turn to ordinary human beings who happen to be strongly and consistently moved by important interests that other people respect, but neglect, and who, for one reason or another, give overt expression to these interests when there is a convenient audience.

As soon as we have recruited these responsible individuals and as soon as we have provided them with facilities and with an audience, we should wait for a moment for the ferment to begin and then gracefully jump clear. Especially for the teacher of the cultural subjects, as opposed to the teacher of technical subjects, we chiefly need to ask that such a teacher give spontaneous expression to the educated man which he finds within himself (Burch, 1957). Surely this is not so uncongenial a chore that a host of security officers is needed to make sure that the teacher applies himself to his job.

Despite its crucial importance, the work of the teacher should not be regarded as neural surgery nor as the manipulation of atomic materials. In teaching, a single technical misstep will seldom spell disaster. As a director of an age-old organic process, the teacher applies his important efforts in more general fashion. He stimulates here, provides nutriment there, and confidently accepts one outcome and rejects another, often enjoying the enviable opportunity of being able to make up tomorrow for the things that were neglected today.

Teachers thus recruited and thus encouraged to vent the free expression of their intellectual interests would constitute an important segment of the environment with which the child would have to reckon or to which he would have to adjust. Hopefully, each child would encounter a variety of teachers. One teacher might be sympathetically and eagerly attuned to the child's interests and concerns. Another might be engrossed not only by the subject matter but by the classroom processes through which his subject matter achieves its impact on the pupil. A third teacher might be exclusively preoccupied with the glories of some subject. For instance, during forty-five minutes each day that he spends in this class, Johnny would have to live with the humbling fact that algebraic truths were considered more important than his own immediate needs.

The relaxation invited by this theory should also extend to the curriculum and to the efforts directed to its reform. The theory would contend that the effective or de facto curriculum is established by the pervasive interests and the active concerns of the teacher. The curricular reforms emanating from the conference room will be effective only insofar as they become incorporated into the concerns that the teacher is led to express. Any statements or decisions coming from the curriculum committee will not be transported intact into the lives of pupils. Such statements must work through a complex chain of interactions.

The original statements of the committee will act as stimuli for one set of people such as subject-matter supervisors. These people, in turn, will react to the stimuli, possibly merely mirroring what they receive, more likely, incorporating much of themselves into the reaction. Their reactions will then act as stimuli for a second set of people who will also react in their own way. After a number of such intermediary transactions, someone, the teacher, will apply some stimuli to the pupil himself.

Of all these modifying human beings, the teacher, of course, is chief. Whatever the truth or persuasiveness of our statements about what to teach, for instance, the teacher's minute-by-minute actions will determine the actual curriculum. Even though our statements elicit the teacher's assent, we cannot be sure that such accepted statements will permeate the hurly-burly of teaching and will function in the momentary interactions that constitute the teaching process.

Since the curricular "message" that we may direct toward the student is to pass through so many people and is to be reinterpreted by each one, it seems unrealistic to strive for precision in the minutia of such statements. It seems hopeless to try to control the teacher's behavior in any detail through a series of messages that we may never recognize by the time they reach him and which may be clearly reorganized by the time they leave him. It would seem wiser, on the contrary, to adopt a more relaxed and general procedure. We should try to decide what the teachers and the schools are likely to do anyway, irrespective of the new forces that we may apply. Knowing what is likely to happen anyway, we can then apply our new efforts in more intelligent fashion.

This lack of precision in determining the curriculum has its encouraging features along with its sobering reminders. When the existing or recent curricula were coming into being, could anyone at that time have foreseen just which features would turn out to be useful to the students of today? What unforeseen gains have come from items that were slipped in despite the complete absence of any pretense of logical justification? What unknown losses have we suffered from items that were excluded on strictly logical grounds? In an area as imprecise as ours, perhaps it is safer to eat "food" as we find it rather than put all our faith in a synthetic diet logically derived from even the most compelling *a priori* principles.

This teacher-centric attitude, stressed throughout the theory, is not motivated primarily by any humanitarian desire to provide the teacher with more autonomy nor to free him from unnecessary nagging anxieties. The emphasis comes, on the contrary, from the claims that the teacher is the crucial factor in the process, that his actual interests determine the effective curriculum, and that his minute-by-minute classroom activities are not susceptible to precise control by others but stem instead from ancient, beneficent tendencies deeply ingrained within him.

As a further implication, we might ask if the theory of spontaneous schooling would minimize the role of professional training in the education of teachers. At the moment: Yes, to some extent. Ultimately: No. For basic or minimal competence in directing an organic process, a clear understanding of the process is not required. Mothers bring forth children, and primitive nurses watch sick people recover, with precious little knowledge of the intricate processes involved. Much effective teaching has been accomplished by people whose knowledge of the learning process was nonexistent or frighteningly erroneous.

At the moment the chief argument for asking teachers to study educational psychology and similar subjects is based on an esthetic rather than a practical imperative. It is repellant and sad to think of an intelligent person regularly immersed in an intriguing and complex process and yet remaining ignorant of the nature of the process. The chauffering housewife, it is true, may remain legitimately (and delightfully) ignorant of what takes place under the hood of the car. However, we would feel sad about a person whose life revolved around cars and yet who had never wondered about the processes that made his work possible. Be that as it may, teachers are bound to theorize about the processes they observe, and if they must theorize, they may be asked to compare their homemade views with other views that have already been propounded and systematized.

There is, of course, the long-range issue. The fact that schooling is regarded as an organic process does not mean that it cannot be improved. Our analogy to agriculture should warn us against unthinkingly adopting that view. True enough, our frantic manipulation of the administrative externals of schooling has produced no such improvement. These efforts have tried to produce improvement while ignoring the humble, basic processes by which schooling proceeds. When we honestly turn to a realistic study of these ancient, earthy, and pervasive forces themselves, who knows what improvement may result? By directing the attention of thousands of teachers to these basic processes and to the principles so far adduced to explain them, we might facilitate a more profound and more relevant understanding of the machinery responsible for schooling and the schools.

REFERENCES

Burch, G. B., The problem of universals in the philosophy of education, *Educ. Theory*, 1957, 7, 216–220.

Churchill, Ruth, and Paula John, Conservation of teaching time through the use of lecture classes and student assistants, *J. educ. Psychol.*, 1958, *49*, 324–327.

Coladarci, A. P., Educational psychology, *Annu. Rev. Psychol.*, 1958, *9*, 189–212.

De Cecco, J. P., Class size and co-ordinated instruction, *Brit. J. educ. Psychol.*, 1964, *34*, 65–74.

Ekstrom, Ruth B., Experimental studies of homogeneous grouping: a critical review, *Sch. Rev.*, 1961, *69*, 216–226.

Feldhusen, J. P., Taps for teaching machines, *Phi Delta Kappan*, 1963, *44*, 265–267.

Fleming, Charlotte M., Class size as a variable in the teaching situation, *Educ. Res.*, 1959, *1*, 35–48.

Gage, N. L., Paradigms for research on teaching, in N. L. Gage, ed., *Handbook of research on teaching.* Skokie, Ill.: Rand McNally, 1963, 94–141.

Ginther, J. R., and W. A. Shrayer, Team teaching in English and history at the eleventh grade level, *Sch. Rev.*, 1962, *70*, 303–313.

Lathrop, I. T., Scholastic achievement at Iowa State College associated with high school size and course pattern, *J. exp. Educ.*, 1960, *29*, 37–48.

McKeachie, W. J., Research on teaching at the college and university level, in N. L. Gage, ed., *Handbook of research on teaching.* Skokie, Ill.: Rand McNally, 1963, 1118–1172.

Merriam, J. L., How well may pupils be prepared for high school work without studying arithmetic, grammar, etc., in the grades? *J. educ. Psychol.*, 1915, *6*, 361–364.

Michelson, J. M., What does research say about effectiveness of the core curriculum?, *Sch. Rev.*, 1957, *65*, 144–160.

Nachman, M., and S. Opochinsky, The effects of different teaching methods: a methodological study, *J. educ. Psychol.*, 1958, *49*, 245–249.

Poppleton, Pamela K., and K. Austwick, A comparison of programmed learning and note-taking at two age levels, *Brit. J. educ. Psychol.*, 1964, *34*, 43–50.

Rice, J. M. The futility of the spelling grind, *The Forum*, 1897, *23*, 163–172.

Schramm, W., Learning from instructional television, *Rev. educ. Res.* 1962, *32*, 156–167.

Stephens, J. M., *The influence of the school upon the individual.* Ann Arbor, Mich.: Edwards Bros., 1933.

Stern, G. G., Measuring noncognitive variables in research on teaching, in N. L. Gage, ed., *Handbook of research on teaching.* Skokie, Ill.: Rand McNally, 1963, 398–447.

White, R. W., How successful is team teaching? *Sci. Teacher*, 1964 (Oct.), *31*, (No. 6), 34–37.

Wiseman, S., Trends in educational psychology, *Brit. J. educ. Psychol.*, 1959, *29*, 128–135.

PART TWO

THE THEORY OF SPONTANEOUS SCHOOLING:

Preliminary Sociological Speculations and a Psychological Analysis

2 | SOME NOTES ON THE GENERAL APPROACH

It will prove necessary at frequent intervals to remind ourselves that this discussion is aimed at an understanding rather than a reform. It is not our immediate aim to improve the schools but to explain how it is that the schools are as good as they are. Such a disinterested approach is by no means usual, and it may be quite disturbing. This, then, is the justification for the frequent reminders that in this study we are not concerned with immediate reform but with the elucidation of a mystery.

It is probably because we are so intimately immersed in the phenomena of schooling that we find it difficult to reconcile ourselves to speculative inquiry in these matters. The problems of schooling press upon us in every aspect of our lives. Many of us are just emerging from the status of pupils within the schools. Others are parents to whom schooling presents itself as a crucial problem. The taxpayer and the responsible citizen also must see the phenomena of schooling not as intriguing intellectual mysteries but as things which primarily demand a practical solution. And to responsible, busy people, sweating over the inescapable practical problems of the day, this invitation to speculative, detached inquiry is likely to appear strange or even wrong.

Our total immersion in the phenomena of schooling not only makes speculative inquiry seem wrong, it also makes such inquiry seem unnecessary. Why bother to explain such familiar phenomena? There is surely no mystery in the fact that schools exist. They exist because we have established them. How do schools achieve their modest results? Obviously, they are achieved through the deliberate efforts of those engaged to teach. Why speculate on matters so self-evident?

Some few educational phenomena, it is true, do strike us as being puzzling or wrong. We may wonder, for instance, at the lowly prestige of the teacher and at the manner in which he is portrayed in literature and drama. Some of the evils we seek to remedy also strike us as being mysterious and offensive not only to the moral conscience but to the intellect as well. One hears, for instance, of a sailor adrift on a life raft who attributes his very survival to the things he learned *while playing truant from school*. This anecdote, when quoted, is likely to be used in criticism of the school and its curriculum. But it may suggest that this misleading emphasis is not only blameworthy but is also mysterious and difficult to understand.

In our approach we shall surely try to explain such errors, but we shall do so by trying to explain the major, more general phenomena of schooling. By doing this we shall find that we have automatically explained these seemingly minor perversities as well.

Schooling Rather than Education

The phenomena to be considered are the phenomena of schooling and not necessarily the more general phenomena of education. Education can be as broad as life itself. Schooling is considered a narrower process linked to a more or less formal institution. Every citizen in his casual actions may inadvertently contribute something to the education of his fellows. The people in the institutions or quasi-institutions known as schools, however, spend much of their time carrying out this function and, by formal designation or common consent, are regarded as having especial responsibility for the younger members of the group.

The Range of the Types of Schools Included

Although concentrating on the narrow phenomenon of schooling, we are by no means concentrating exclusively on the contemporary school of western culture. We should get a much clearer picture of the proposed mechanisms of schooling, as a matter of fact, if we turn our attention away from the highly organized schools of western Europe or the United States and turn it toward the primitive schools of some earlier times or toward some so-called primitive cultures in our own day. A theory that adequately explains these examples of more primitive schools should have no difficulty in making sense out of the gleaming computer-run establishments of today.

Type of Explanation Attempted

In the general discussion of our approach, there is much emphasis on *explaining* the phenomena of schooling or on *making sense out of* those phenomena. For our purpose an explanation simply consists of a small set of statements which, for the time being, must be taken for granted and from which the facts to be explained could be deduced. Let us suppose, for instance, that the facts to be explained consist of an assortment of barks, hisses, sputterings, and growls coming from the front of a house. To *explain* the facts thus described, someone suggests that a dog has chased the neighbor's cat under the porch. This simple comment has many of the characteristics of a true explanation. In the first place, it is a statement from which the facts described could be deduced. Knowing about the chase and about certain unexpressed but familiar characteristics of dogs and cats, we would expect the noises that we have just heard.

We should note also that the statement in this explanation is somewhat broader than the particular facts described. Not only could these particular facts be deduced from the general explanatory statement, but we could deduce other actual or imminent facts. We could expect, for instance, that if we looked under the porch we would see the two animals addressing each other in their respective ways. We could estimate the probabilities that the cat would later emerge in a certain characteristic manner.

It is of the greatest importance that our explanatory statements should cover more than the immediate phenomena they are intended to explain. Otherwise we would end up with a separate explanation for each phenomenon. Critics of the older instinct theory, for instance, have held that each time an unexplained phenomenon was observed, one merely had to concoct a new instinct to take care of the problem. Similarly, people engaged in curve-fitting may achieve success by supplying a separate constant for each point that the curve should reach. In both instances, little is accomplished. We still have to make a separate statement or substatement for each fact to be described or explained.

In its stress on tendencies, the present theory will probably invite comparison with the instinct theory just mentioned. The tendencies used here have much in common with some concepts of instinct. Consequently, the theory, even at the outset, may seem to invite the whole undifferentiated bag of criticisms that, at one time or another, have been directed to the general instinct theory.

The current theory can plead a resounding "not guilty" to one charge frequently levelled at the instinct theory. The current view cannot be accused of achieving its success by endlessly multiplying or manufacturing additional explanatory terms. It has rashly attempted to derive a vast number of separate phenomena from very few explanatory terms. The inevitable corrections that await this theory will surely come from an elaboration and extension of these few explanatory terms and not from a reduction in their number.

The explanatory statements should be smaller in number than the events they profess to describe. It is also a help if those statements are of a kind that we can accept or take for granted, for the time being at least. Sometimes these postulated entities fit in with our ordinary experience and are extremely easy to accept. It is rather natural, for instance, to assume that a force acting on an object will tend to make the object move. A minor phenomenon convincingly deduced from this assumption becomes shorn of its mystery. At other times, however, the statements that we are asked to take for granted are by no means so immediately compelling. These statements, for instance, may ask us to visualize a fourth, fifth, or nth dimension. Such explanations bring intellectual assent but may fail to carry the comforting conviction that we often value. This prized feeling of, "Aha! Yes! Now I understand," is likely to arise only when the parent principles from which the facts are to be derived are themselves so familiar or so seemingly axiomatic as to have been purged of all bewilderment.

Fortunately, as it happens, in this undertaking the master principles which serve as our explanation and which we are asked to take for granted are neither strange nor formidable. Our explanation is to be derived from a few statements about some widespread human tendencies that are very familiar and earthy indeed. We try to show that if these tendencies did exist they would account for the things that go on in contemporary schools. Such forces or tendencies, we also contend, would account for the surprising constancy of the school's achievements in the face of stupendous efforts to modify those achievements.

The approach to be employed here will operate on two rather distinct levels. On one level there will be a serious, intensive effort to apply the theory to the contemporary work of the school and to the well-documented data bearing on the work of the school. This, obviously, is the proper job of the educational psychologist.

In a tentative way at least, the theory will go beyond educational psychology. Along with its application to the hard data of educational psychology, the theory also has applications to broader social phenomena, phenomena that properly concern the student of social evolution. In its broader and more ambitious aspects, the theory holds that the same forces, here postulated to account for the contemporary work of the school, are also able to explain the general social role of the school. The broader theory holds, in fact, that the same forces needed to explain the work of the contemporary school would also account for the very existence of schooling in the first place. These same forces would explain the school's traditional concentration on some areas of life and its relative neglect of others. This aspect of the theory, going far beyond the realm of educational psychology, cannot be developed here in any detail or with any precision. The broader aspects of the theory are still there, however, and will continue to be discovered in the background. At times, moreover, these broader aspects will play an explicit part in the argument. This broader theory, moreover, forms the larger structure which includes the more detailed and business-like development. All in all, it would seem best if the more general theory were given explicit treatment, however sketchily and however tentatively.

In this venture into the world of anthropology and social evolution, we shall not, of course, make any pretence of dealing with clearly established historical or anthropological data. We appeal, on the contrary, to a more or less imaginary set of observations having only a rough and approximate resemblance to the actual events. In this procedure we follow the lead of many psychologists who have to make assumptions about the hidden facts of neurology. Rather than attempt a meticulous matching of their assumptions with the complex and uncertain data of neurology, these psychologists invoke a *conceptual nervous system,* so frequently the subject of humorous comment.

This procedure of setting up a largely hypothetical state of affairs may not be so foolish or so futile as it has been made to sound. We bring out many aspects of the theory itself in applying the theory to even a hypothetical world. The use of such make-believe structures also permits some preliminary testing of a theory even before the mythical universe is compared to its factual counterpart. It might be useful, for instance, to see if the proposed theory could be consistently applied to the purely schematic world that had been set up. True enough, consistency within this schematic world would not be proof of a consistent match with the real world. Inconsistency within the conjectured world, however, would have more definite implications and thus might permit us to eliminate an unpromising theory even in the absence of hard data.

3 | THE ORIGINS AND SOCIAL ROLE OF THE SCHOOL: A Speculative Account

This chapter and the next represent an exceedingly broad canvas on which we try to rough out, in general fashion, the setting in which the specific forces of schooling may have developed. After showing, in these two chapters, how our basic forces may have developed by broad evolutionary demand, we turn, in Chapter 5, to the more specific data of the contemporary school. At that point the broad schematic approach is abandoned and the search for relevant data becomes extremely business-like.

Having thus been given warning of the speculative and schematic nature of the discussion to follow, we should now feel free to move in quite positive fashion. Speculations or hypotheses, clearly announced as such, can properly be stated in quite dogmatic terms, in fact, the more flat-footed the utterance, the more clear-cut the discrepancies that it may contain.

Schools exist and, in varying degrees of "schoolness," have existed through many eras and in many cultures. Such schools or near-schools, moreover, have addressed themselves largely to an identifiable group of tasks. In any culture, for instance, there are some jobs that would instantly be recognized as appropriate for the school. Other tasks would seem less appropriate.

This phenomenon of schooling cannot be defined in categorical fashion. As has been suggested, there are varying degrees of "schoolness." Activities vary in the degree to which the label of "school" would be appropriate. With the mother-child dyad, the term would not seem appropriate at all. When the older sister substitutes for the mother, we get some vague hint of schooling. The school as envisaged here would include the extended family in which training is provided by uncles and grandparents. The term "school" becomes even more appropriate when the solicitous outsider directs the play of children or has them listen to tribal legends. The term becomes more and more appropriate as the adults involved become less and less identified with the biological parents, as the contacts between these adults and the children become more sustained, and as their responsibilities to the children become more clearly formalized. It is of the utmost importance to the theory that the concept of school should not be limited to the highly elaborate institutions of the present day, but the concept involved should be seen as extending, although with diminished force, to the very doorstep of the parent-child dyad.

What forces could have led other people to supplement the nurture provided by the primitive mother? What forces, especially, could have led to the more elaborate institutions that represent the beginnings of schools? If we had to start all over again, what forces would we have to set in motion to guarantee the emergence of schools, simple or elaborate, and to make sure that these schools would direct their attentions to a definable area?

To distinguish between the tasks that the school has undertaken and those other tasks which it has ignored, we should examine a group of human tendencies or ways of behaving. We should ask about the survival value of those tendencies. We should ask especially whether the survival value of any tendency is immediate or more remote.

Tendencies and Their Survival Value

As used here, the concept of *tendency*, or *way of behaving*, merely refers to some identifiable way of doing things. We would like to be able to say, for instance, that most people have a tendency to sneeze upon sniffing pepper; that one person, Jimmie Jones, has a tendency to cry when his wagon upsets; or that another person, Mr. Jones, has a tendency to turn to the editorial page immediately upon opening the newspaper. Each of these brief descriptions represents a tendency or a way of behaving. It is something that can be identified. Its probability of occurrence (high or low) can be estimated.

For the purpose of this discussion, tendencies or ways of behaving are merely descriptive labels. In using these terms, nothing whatever is implied about many highly controversial matters, such as the underlying neural processes, the permanence or variability of the tendency, or the amount of deliberation that goes into the behavior. The tendencies to be considered may range from those responsible for a blink of the eye to those responsible for a declaration of war. The concept includes, at one extreme, behavior that is instigated by the prick of a pin and, at the other, behavior that is brought about by a closely reasoned conviction of impending ruin. It includes behavior that terminates with a simple movement, as well as behavior that terminates only with the attainment of a long-held objective. We shall consider some ways of behaving that seem to reflect a definite purpose, and other behavior that the psychiatrist may attribute to an unconscious motive, and still other behavior that may seem completely devoid of conscious purpose.

Many of these ways of behaving are classified according to the biological (or survival) function that they serve. For instance, we talk about reproductive tendencies and tendencies concerned with food-getting. In so labelling or classifying these tendencies, however, we do not wish to imply that the person himself is always, or typically, conscious of the biological function of his behavior. Tendencies are labelled food-getting, not because they are always accompanied or governed by the desire to secure nourishment, but because that is the biological result that they actually do achieve.

Survival value, as discussed here, must be used in a very broad sense. With intensive analysis (Kallen, 1966), the concept proves to be somewhat fuzzy or ambiguous. In respect to the schools, for instance, just what can be considered to survive? Is it biological germ plasm, a set of ideas, or some combination of descendants and ideas? Does the term "failure to survive" apply to ancient Egypt in the same sense that it applies to Cro-Magnon man?

With all its imprecision, the concept of survival value seems useful in a general way. There is a very real fact that Inca civilization no longer flourishes. There is also the fact that the societies of western Europe have become influential through a number of generations. Broadly, we can say merely that a tendency has survival value if, in sustained fashion, it results in the transmission of something which enables the recipient group to hold its own in competition with other groups.

Used in this very general sense, survival value has been the concept traditionally invoked to account for the fact that a species is equipped with a certain tendency. We feel no need, for instance, to ask why people have a tendency to eat when hungry or why the members of various species tend to nurture their young. It is true that we may feel much curiosity regarding the precise mechanisms by which they are handed on from one generation to another, but we are not puzzled by the fact that they are present. It is only when we encounter tendencies that have no obvious survival value that we feel impelled to account for the existence of those tendencies. At times, for instance, there has been some urge to account for play tendencies or for the more frivolous manipulative tendencies. The explanations proffered, moreover, typically try to show that the seemingly "useless" tendencies really have a survival function (the approach taken here), or that they can be derived from tendencies that do have substantial survival value.

Differences in the Immediacy of Survival Value

It is probable that all widespread tendencies are linked in some way with survival value. It is probable that such tendencies either currently contribute to our survival or are derived from some tendency that once had, or now has, survival value. It would seem unlikely that the race has carried along with it on its evolutionary journey many tendencies that have not proved of value in one way or another.

Although we can assume that all well-established tendencies, or traits, have had some evolutionary value, we must not infer that the survival value of each of these is equally immediate or direct. Some tendencies, such as those involved in breathing, may have a survival value that is extremely immediate. The loss of such behavior would ordinarily result in immediate disaster. For many other traits, however, the survival value, though still marked, clearly is more remote. Gregarious behavior, for instance, probably contributes greatly to survival, but it must do so in this more remote fashion. A species deprived of the tendencies responsible for this behavior might well persist for some years, or even for generations.

To get a more down-to-earth view of this concept of "immediacy of survival value," let us suppose that for each of a number of traits we ask the following question: If this trait, or tendency, had been eliminated during the development of the species or group, how long would the group have survived? Notice that the emphasis is on group survival. Many tendencies might result in the extinction of the individual but might be important to the survival of the group. Using the estimates that we might reach, let us place these tendencies, or groups of tendencies, on a gradient ranging from immediate survival value, at one extreme, to very remote survival value, at the other. Figure 3.1 provides a list of some arbitrarily selected tendencies. On the base line, breathing is placed well toward the left. This means that, had the species lost the tendency to breathe, the time left to that species would be very short indeed. The tendency to drop stones in water, on the other hand, is placed well toward the right. A species deprived of the tendencies responsible for this behavior may still have struggled on for thousands of years.

The particular tendencies appearing along the gradient have been selected for illustrative purposes only. They are quite arbitrary, and their placement on the gradient is by no means intended to be precise or universal.

Figure 3.1.

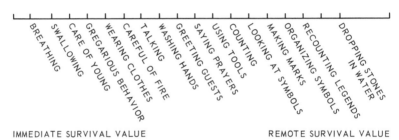

IMMEDIATE SURVIVAL VALUE   REMOTE SURVIVAL VALUE

GRADIENT OF REMOTENESS OF SURVIVAL VALUE

The tendency to drop stones in water is used as one illustration of the large number of frivolous, manipulative tendencies that are so prominent in human and primate make-up. Thorndike spoke of them as the tendency to "be a cause." Harlow has stressed the part they play in the process of learning in monkeys (Harlow and McClearn, 1954). Educational psychologists (Stephens, 1951) have urged teachers not to neglect the value in these playful tendencies. Recently, White (1959) has included such "result-getting" tendencies in his idea of competence as a motive.

It is possible, of course, that one may wonder if these frivolous, playful, or decorative tendencies have any survival value whatever, immediate or otherwise. Is there any survival value whatever, for instance, in the infant's tendency to bang spoons on tables or to crumple paper? What survival value is there in the tendency of the older child to make marks on walls or to smash milk bottles on the pavement? What survival value is there in the tendency of his elders to finger a lock of hair, to doodle on margins of note books, to slam away at golf balls, or to rearrange ideas?

Arguing directly against these feelings of doubt, we shall claim much survival value, however remote, for these playful tendencies. All in all, these seemingly frivolous tendencies which nature permitted our ancestors to carry along—which, indeed, she may have insisted that they carry along—have been far from useless. In the long run, these playful, decorative tendencies have had inestimable value for the groups or species possessing them. Many of our great discoveries and advances have come from these fiddling, meddling, and monkeying tendencies. A species lacking these tendencies would never have stumbled, and explored, and bungled its way into the discoveries that have given our species its current preeminence. Our great advances have come from men who idly sketched in sand or on rocks and who thereby stumbled upon written communication. Other gains have come from men who were playfully intrigued by the noisy disruption of hot rocks immersed in cold water or from people who amused themselves with the resonance of a hollow log and who thereby stumbled upon a surprisingly efficient signalling device.

There is no expectation that each and every one of these frivolous tendencies will ultimately turn out to have substantial survival value. Of the many seemingly "useless" tendencies that we now cultivate, only one or two later may aid our descendants in their struggle to survive. Furthermore, there should be no expectation that we can now select the group, or class, from which those tendencies with future value will be drawn. For all we know, they may come from something that now seems as fantastic and absurd as Godard's rocket experiments seemed some fifty years ago. Some later group, for instance, may find the key to survival in the development of telepathic hypnosis, or from the prolonged study of the cave life of bats, or in some other weird activity that now elicits jeers or amusement.

It is not necessary to suggest that each and every one of these tendencies to the right of the gradient will ultimately pay off. It is only necessary to assume that, in the long run, some few of these tendencies, if adequately developed, will give one society an advantage over societies that have no means of developing them.

We have made much of the seemingly frivolous or playful nature of some of these tendencies with remote survival value. There are many such activities with remote survival value, however, that are pursued in earnest. Lee (1961) lays great stress on the tremendous exertions of Eskimos and of Hopi Indians to achieve artistic or ritualistic results that can have no immediate survival value. In a later section we show that the school has given its chief attention to those remote activities that can be elaborated and systematized. As soon as they come under the special concern of the school, such activities are often regarded in a manner that is far from playful. The essential characteristic of these activities is their lack of immediate survival value and not the degree of seriousness with which the performer or his audience regards them.

Mechanisms to Provide
for Adequate Development

If tendencies such as those indicated in Figure 3.1 are to contribute to survival, each must reach a stage of development which permits it to function. Each tendency must be developed to the point where it can actually play a part in survival. By what means is this development assured? Can we identify any general mechanisms that could insure an effective degree of development for tendencies in different portions of the gradient?

To suggest how this necessary nurture might be accomplished, we show in Figure 3.2 how different mechanisms may take care of the different tendencies that vary in the immediacy of their survival value. The upper boundary of Figure 3.2 represents the degree of development that any tendency must attain if it is to contribute to survival. To bring each tendency up to this level, several different mechanisms may play a part.

Naturally enough, for the development of the tendencies most urgently needed for survival, nature has provided devices that are as foolproof as possible. For basic competence in such tendencies as breathing or swallowing, for instance, there is little dependence on anything as precarious as experience, learning, or intelligence. True, these tendencies profit to some extent from learning, but, for the most part, learning plays only a minor role. For tendencies with such crucial biological importance, a good deal of proficiency is practically guaranteed by reflexes or by other direct physiological processes. Some of these tendencies are almost completely ready to function at the time of birth. Others may not develop until later but seem to wait only for a period of maturation.

The heavy curve to the left of Figure 3.2 is intended to show that maturation is almost self-sufficient for the adequate development of traits at the extreme left of the gradient. For these tendencies, only a slight contribution from any other mechanism is necessary to supplement the influence of this primitive maturation.

Although the maturation of inherent tendencies is able, almost unaided, to guarantee basic competence in breathing and sucking, it is by no means self-sufficient for developing those tendencies by which children deal with dangerous objects, wear adequate clothing, or avoid the wrath of their elders. The primitive force of maturation must be supplemented by some other mechanism if these tendencies are to be developed to the point of effectiveness.

As maturation comes to be less and less adequate in guaranteeing the necessary degree of development, it is held to be supplemented by the urgent spontaneous concerns of parents. In this connection it is neces-

Figure 3.2. Mechanisms available to induce adequate development of tendencies that vary in the remoteness of survival value.

LEVEL OF DEVELOPMENT NECESSARY TO PLAY A PART IN SURVIVAL

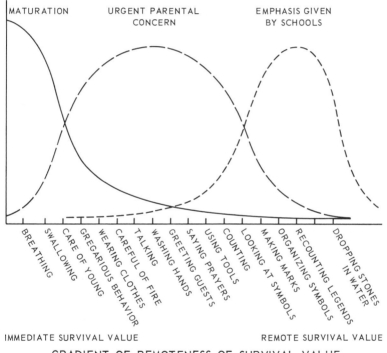

IMMEDIATE SURVIVAL VALUE   REMOTE SURVIVAL VALUE

GRADIENT OF REMOTENESS OF SURVIVAL VALUE

sary to distinguish between those things, at one extreme, for which the home feels an *immediate, urgent,* and *continuous* concern, and those other things, at the other extreme, for which the home feels only *remote, indulgent,* or *sporadic* concern.

This contrast in concern is illustrated by the different attitudes that most of us take toward a break in the plumbing, on the one hand, and toward a dwindling bank account, on the other. Both elicit concern.

Either may spell disaster. Accordingly, the burst plumbing, by its very nature, will demand and get immediate attention, whereas the threat of gradual insolvency may elicit nothing more than a resolve to take care of the matter is the future.

Within the home, the activities of children vary in the urgency with which they demand attention. As with the burst plumbing, for instance, the child's failure to dress himself before wandering down the street may elicit immediate and positive action. His tendency to confuse the words "was" and "saw," on the other hand, although quite worrisome, may elicit a different kind of parental concern. This concern, similar to the concern felt for the dwindling bank account, expresses itself in less immediate or positive fashion. It may well be one of those things that should be looked after at a future date.

It is this urgent, spontaneous parental concern that first provides nurture for those traits which would be incompletely served by maturation. As the role of maturation ceases to be completely effective, the role of urgent parental concern, as represented by the middle curve in Figure 3.2, comes more and more to represent the major force.

Urgent parental concern, though the chief custodian of traits in the middle range of the gradient, cannot be depended upon to continue at a high level throughout the entire range. After a point, urgent parental concern begins to decline. For many traits at the right of the gradient, the combined influence of maturation and of parental concern would no longer supply the nurture necessary for adequate development. If left to nothing but maturation and to spontaneous parental concern, for instance, the tendency to manipulate symbols would seldom be developed to the point where it could make any contribution to survival.

It has been the unique function of the school to provide the necessary nurture for many of the tendencies not adequately cultivated by other agencies. For some of these tendencies with remote and sporadic survival value, the traditional school has shown marked concern and has thus nurtured many traits which, otherwise, would have been neglected. The dashed curve to the right of the gradient in Figure 3.2 suggests that this concern of the traditional school plays an increasing part as the more primitive concern of the home begins to decline. Thus, for a certain number of traits to the right of the gradient, varying of course from society to society and from century to century, a reasonable degree of development is assured.

There has been considerable stress on the fact that the school supplies nurture for only a certain number of these traits to the right of the gradient, and these favored traits vary from culture to culture and from one era to another. Although this matter cannot be discussed in detail, it still seems wise to suggest first, that some of this selection may be due to mere accident, tradition, or to the establishment of vocal groups with vested interests, and, second, that a supplementary gradient of *elaborateness* seems to be at work. By this gradient of elaborateness, we suggest that the school is more likely to favor these "remote" traits that are elaborate, verbal, and systematic as opposed to those that are simple, manual, and haphazard. The school is more likely, for instance, to deal with the arrangement of ideas than with the act of throwing stones into the water. It is possible, of course, that there is additional survival value in this supplementary emphasis on systematic, generalized, symbolic manipulations. So long as the school is going to concentrate on matters with remote survival value, there may be a higher yield from the more general, the more persisting, and the more universally applicable activities.

These, however, are minor variations in an otherwise consistent pattern. By and large the school nurtures those tendencies which the home neglects in its minute-by-minute, urgent concerns, limiting itself to a remote, sporadic or indulgent concern. Essentially the school has evolved as an agency that shows as much day-by-day concern for writing and for tribal legends as the home has shown for the more vital matters of eating and talking.

In fostering and nurturing these more decorative and less vital aspects of behavior, the school, unwittingly perhaps, has played a substantial part in the grim struggle for survival between one society and another. By concentrating on a vast number of these seemingly "useless" things, such as topology or electrostatics, and by inducing generation after generation to become familiar with the various nuances of the "scholastic" subjects, the school has helped develop a few of the seemingly "useless" things to the point of tremendous practical return. Consequently, the school has occasionally given its host society a terrific advantage over societies that refuse to tolerate dilettantism or the pursuit of the impractical. Whatever its other virtues, the school has been a survival device which some societies evolved, or borrowed, or stumbled upon, or otherwise acquired during the remote past.

In stressing the survival value of the school's specialized concern, we must not for a moment suggest that the school has been aware of the survival advantages in its specialized work. Nor has it had a clear idea of the remote, but problematic, survival value in the various traits on which it lavishes its care. On the contrary, we find that, for the most part, when these activities are cultivated, they are typically cultivated as ends in themselves. To the artist and his patrons, art is not just one of many activities that might happen to have practical value centuries from now. Art, to its devotees, has its own essential value, not derivable from its potential utility, and is to be cultivated for the satisfaction of intrinsic human needs. As with disinterested science, it is considered to be valuable for its own sake.

Not only is it a fact that "useless" activities bring rich and genuine satisfaction in their own right, quite apart from their remote survival value, but that they should do so is most helpful. Activities which bring direct and powerful satisfactions in and of themselves are more likely to be carried on with zeal and efficiency than those which are undertaken merely from a sense of duty to future generations. The continuation of the species, for instance, is more likely to be guaranteed through pro-creative activities which are enjoyable or attractive in their own right than through a sheer sense of obligation to acquire progeny.

Mechanisms Responsible for the Evolution of Schools

In view of the long-term survival value inherent in schools and in their special interests, it is not surprising that schools have evolved or developed in many societies. But this is merely to say that schools would turn out to be useful or convenient once they did evolve. We may still feel some curiosity about the processes which produced these useful institutions. If we were to re-enact this evolution, for instance, what sort of mechanisms would we need to have?

It would be natural to suppose that societies established schools in the same way that they dug wells or built walls. They saw the advantages of such facilities and deliberately set out to attain them.

But there are difficulties in attributing the development of schools exclusively to rational, deliberate decisions. For one thing, it is unlikely that the early societies were able to see the extremely remote survival value that lay in their nurture of playful, decorative tendencies which we find to the right of our gradient. In accounting for any phenomenon really vital to survival, moreover, we should be wary about placing undue reliance on deliberate rational decisions. Keeping in mind the school's role in survival, we may well wonder if the continuation of these survival-favoring features has, in the past, depended *exclusively* on anything as precarious as human deliberation. Deliberate intellectual decisions, which are assumed to play so important a part in our current civilized life, are probably of very recent origin and, even now, are not very reassuring guarantees for the continuation of anything really vital to survival. If we are to explain the school's contribution to survival during the remote periods of the past, we should look for some of the responsible forces in a group of blind, primitive tendencies which op-erated to produce schools prior to the development of elaborate deliberation and which have operated successfully under extremely diverse rationales. To provide a convincing explanation of the schools, we must place some of our reliance on forces which will work when deliberation is inadequate or nonexistent—which will work, indeed, even when deliberation is perversely obstructional.

The basic forces that have led to the evolution of the school and have kept it at work in survival-favoring channels are to be found not only in human deliberation but to a great extent in a few clusters of widespread, primitive, spontaneous tendencies that frequently owe little to deliberate decision.

The first of these clusters of spontaneous tendencies consists of the *manipulative tendencies* that occupy the right-hand range of Figure 3.2. These tendencies, it will be remembered, include such things as doodling, making marks in the sand, exploiting an echo, playing with word patterns, and working out numerical relations.

Along with these spontaneous manipulative tendencies, we also postulate spontaneous *communicative tendencies*. There is a cluster of spontaneous communicative tendencies which lead us *to talk to other people about our interests*. Here the emphasis is not on our deliberate efforts to help or improve the hearer but on our spontaneous descriptions of our travels, our operations, our pets, our achievements, and of the various things that we happen to know.

In other clusters we see tendencies that lead us, on the one hand, to *applaud* or *commend*, in spontaneous fashion, some performances of people and lead us, on the other hand, to express *disapproval* of other performances, or to *correct* an inappropriate performance, or to *show discomfort* on its occurrence. Here, again, we do not refer to the conscious, altruistic efforts to encourage other people or to increase their competence but to the spontaneous, automatic smile or applause, to the uncontrolled grimace, or to the spontaneous, unthinking correction that springs to our lips when we hear a word mispronounced or detect a factual error.

Among the cluster of tendencies that lead us to speak of what we know, we should give some attention to a special cluster by which we are led to *supply the answer for which someone else is groping*. This, again, refers not to quiet and kindly aid supplied upon request but to the compulsive blurting out of information even when our aid is quite unwelcome.

Closely related to the urges to supply the answer, are those that spontaneously lead us *to point the moral*, to call attention to the things that follow from a given course of action. Without thinking about the matter we say, "See how much better things are now that you do it this way!" "See what happens when you don't watch where you are going!" We see a connection between a certain way of behaving and a certain result. Seeing this we are compelled to announce our discovery. Often we do so even in the face of a deliberate resolve to remain silent.

Along with these active, positive tendencies, we must postulate a cluster of tendencies, or inhibitions, that lead us to *tolerate certain kinds of behavior in others*. We must have some basis for tolerating the person excessively endowed with the manipulative tendencies and the various communicative tendencies.

Our main task is to show that, to some extent, schooling would arise from the blind, automatic operation of a group of nondeliberate, spontaneous tendencies such as those just postulated. It is now necessary to show that the clusters of tendencies are fairly widespread, though, of course, much more pronounced in some people than in others; that such tendencies will operate even without deliberate, conscious intention to help, to instruct, or to improve; and that such tendencies, even if unaided by deliberate intention, would bring about some of the phenomena of schooling.

Prevalence and Spontaneity of the Postulated Tendencies

The frivolous, playful, result-getting tendencies are extremely widespread. They are found in our primate cousins and in human beings of all ages. The young child crumples papers and topples blocks with obvious relish. His older brother smashes light bulbs or sends rocks skimming over the surface of the pond. Other members of the species send balls soaring through space or delight in the results obtained from manipulating lures near pools or streams. At a more "intellectual" level, many people rearrange the letters in words, do interesting mathematical puzzles, or develop ingenious theories on a wide variety of subjects.

The tendencies to hold forth on a variety of subjects are also very widespread, though these tendencies are also much more pronounced in some people than in others. With little persuasion, most people will speak to some extent about themselves, about their family, their hobbies, or their views, and some people will speak interminably on such topics.

The tendencies to approve or applaud manipulative behavior in others are also fairly prevalent and are probably very ancient. Most people are impressed by some form of manipulatory skill when they see it in others; for example, the acrobat, the medicine man, and the storyteller have enjoyed prestige among many different groups.

The tendencies to express dismay, consternation, or disapproval at the awkward or incorrect manipulative behavior of others are also widespread and are again much more strongly entrenched in some people than in others. The prevalence of this tendency is perhaps shown by the deliberate efforts often applied to keep it in check. Rules and sanctions are continually enjoined to keep us from gasping at the overturned teacup, from commenting on our friend's inappropriate attire, or from correcting his faulty grammar.

Equally widespread are the tendencies to supply the answer for which someone else is groping. This is the spontaneous urge the director of the quiz program tries to suppress when he pleads for no prompting. It is the urge behind the frantic hand-waving of pupils as they rush to give the answer that eludes one of their colleagues.

The tendency to point the moral, to say, "I told you so," again, is frequently seen among us. As with some of the tendencies just mentioned, it is, in fact, so much a part of our make-up that many societies have erected taboos against it.

The tolerating processes are not so obvious or conspicuous, but they must be assumed to exist. Some kind of tolerating must have been present to permit the free indulgence of the manipulative activities. The hard pressed primitive groups may well have questioned the social contribution of the curious individual who amused himself by throwing water on hot rocks or who toyed with a rope-like vine when he could have been shaping flints or chasing rabbits. Not being seers, they could not foretell that the playful one was about to revolutionize the method of working rocks or of snaring rabbits. Forbearance for triflers must have come hard to those sweating over the immediate tasks of the day. Nevertheless such forbearance did come about in some species, and it greatly helped such species to utilize the long-term survival value of these frivolous, manipulatory tendencies. Certainly, some toleration is quite prevalent in societies that survive at the moment.

Beyond mere tolerance comes the active approval and applause for manipulatory activities. The group which first carried its indulgent forbearance into spontaneous encouragement was also the first to take one more step toward the effective utilization of the survival value latent in these traits. The group who found themselves, for some strange reason, intrigued by the playful exploits of others, by the tales of the poet, or by the magic of the medicine man, would be more likely to survive than groups which gave mere grudging acceptance. This trait, too, is very widespread.

As has been suggested, toleration for the unusually "communicative" person is sometimes of a grudging nature. Typically we are not too happy when we ourselves must listen to a detailed account of our companion's esoteric hobbies, or when he comments on our own manipulatory deficiencies, or when he sharpens our insight into the reasons for our ineptitude. But we are more indulgent, or perhaps moderately enthusiastic, when the one who abounds with information, corrections, or maxims applies himself to others, especially if those others stand in obvious need of the treatment being given. Presumably, even in primitive groups, there was some forbearance, or perhaps support, for the oldster who took advantage of the more defenseless members of the group by telling them of the old days, by correcting their off-key chant, or by showing them how a violation of the tribal law brings its own retribution.

Do these tendencies operate spontaneously? Would they function adequately in a group of people who lacked any conception of the survival value of such tendencies? Probably so. Probably the boy who rattles the stick along the paling fence has no idea that this is one of the tendencies by which his species has fiddled and doodled its way into its present preeminence and by which his descendants may achieve even more fantastic control of the environment. The man who is impelled to give you a detailed account of the book he has read is also probably completely oblivious of the fact that this urge has long-range survival value. The spectator who gazes in awe at the colored magic which the priest can induce in the campfire does not know that his appreciation or applause also pushes his species a little ahead of less effusive groups. The adult who feels impelled to correct the child's off-key chant probably does so as blindly as do the rest. He merely feels uncomfortable in the presence of improper manipulation, and he acts. In so doing, he helps perpetuate manipulative tendencies which in some distant day may mean salvation for his descendants. But of this he probably knows nothing. The society which tolerates or encourages this primitive teacher also thereby adds to the long-time chances of survival; again it probably does so with little realization that the encouragement has survival value.

It is not suggested that these activities are always completely lacking in deliberation. It is obvious that people may talk of their hobbies or their interests for the deliberate purpose of helping their hearers or of accomplishing some other laudable aim. The man who tells you all about his operation, for instance, may believe that he can pass along some information that may be useful to you. However, this is not always the case or necessarily the case. Sometimes he just babbles. He is driven by some undeliberate, unintellectual tendency to talk, and he talks. He is sometimes the victim of that spontaneous, unreasoning drive which leads the returning traveller, even as the gangplank falls, to look frantically for a pair of ears into which he can pour forth his experiences. He may merely belong to that group of people for whom an unshared experience is no experience at all. A story heard but untold leaves him in acute distress. It must be remembered that this spontaneous compulsion to tell others the things we know is much stronger in some people than in others. Most of us could sort our acquaintances into rough ranks with respect to this trait. At the one extreme is the friend whom we avoid for some time after he has returned from his trip. We make a point not to lunch with him the day after he has been to the theater. We hope the book he has just read is interesting—and brief. At the other extreme is the unduly "secretive" person, the partaker of the solitary, intellectual delights. Most of us probably come somewhere between these two extremes.

The tendency to correct the mistakes of others may also, upon occasion, spring from a deliberate intention to help the erring individual. Again this is not always true or necessarily true. In the margins of books that no one else will ever see, we write corrections to authors already dead. We correct spelling errors in examination books that will never be returned. Many of our corrections are probably devoid of deliberate, rational intention to help. Often there is absolutely nothing altruistic about them. We hear the mistake and, spontaneously—automatically—helplessly, wince, or supply the correct phrase, or shriek in outraged protest. Even when we feel that our comment may hurt rather than help, we are sometimes powerless to resist, and the spontaneous tendency to comment on the mistake wins out in the face of a deliberate resolve to mind our own business.

In this trait, as in the others, we may expect marked individual differences. At the one extreme are those who just cannot keep quiet in the presence of error, irrespective of the harm or good that may follow from speaking out, and at the other extreme are those who can be aware of serious dereliction and feel no compulsion whatever to speak or correct.

The Power of the Postulated Tendencies to Produce Schooling

If we grant the existence of these spontaneous tendencies, together with the individual differences that are also postulated, then something similar to schooling seems inevitable. From among those who are unusually endowed with manipulative tendencies, there would be some who are also strongly compelled to speak of what they know. Such people would tend to direct their efforts to any available audience. It would be amazing, however, if a disproportionate part of their hearers did not happen to be drawn from those too young or too timid to escape. Children constitute a natural captive audience of this kind, especially if there is in the background the indulgent permission or blessing of parents. The ancient mariner may well have "shared his experiences" with accessible eight-year olds if all the startled wedding guests had succeeded in giving him the slip.

Among the adults who are unthinkingly impelled to hold forth on "academic" matters, there would be some who, driven by similar blind, unreasoning compulsions, would also commend behavior that pleased them and correct those things that worried them. Many of these, in turn, would be spontaneously impelled to point the moral, to show why this result follows from that way of doing things, and to supply the answer that may elude the "pupils."

The activities just outlined constitute a crude form of schooling. Here, for instance, we have the adult who, because of his own great interest in tribal history, talks to young people about tribal history. His remarks occasionally lead them to express themselves on the same subject. Some of their remarks he unthinkingly accepts and others he rejects. Such an individual has taken a considerable step toward the teaching of tribal history, even though he may never have had the slightest intention to teach.

To the student of a social phenomenon such as schooling, these powerful, primitive tendencies that motivate the snail watcher, the bore, and the compulsive "corrector" must neither be taken lightly nor brushed aside as merely interesting or laughable human foibles. These tendencies, so prevalent and so characteristic of our species, have enabled our ancestors to develop a host of seemingly "useless" "academic" activities to the point where a few of these tendencies have produced tremendous survival returns. It is claimed that these blind, primitive forces are exceedingly dependable agencies for nurturing such academic matters and for capturing their sporadic, long-range survival value.

No attempt has been made to work out the detailed mechanisms by which these postulated tendencies have been handed on. *In general,* of course, our possession of these traits is adequately explained by the fact that the societies who happened to be endowed with these clusters of tendencies were able, in the long run, to "out-compete" the societies who lacked such tendencies.

These clusters of primitive tendencies, so clearly prevalent in our day and presumably prevalent in the past, would provide the basic forces necessary for a crude form of schooling. Those blind, undeliberate forces, at work in the past, would do much to account for the continuity of schooling and for its prevalence in different cultures. These steady, primitive tendencies, still functioning in our more elaborate schools, would also account for a certain constancy in the tasks undertaken by the schools in spite of widely differing rationales, justifications, or deliberate pressures.

REFERENCES

Harlow, H. F., and G. E. McClearn, Object discrimination learned by monkeys on the basis of manipulation motives, *J. comp. physiol. Psychol.*, 1954, *47*, 73–76.

Kallen, H. M., Education as survival, *Educ. Theory*, 1966, *16*, 71–84.

Lee, Dorothy, Autonomous motivations, in F. C. Geuber, ed., *Anthropology and education*. Philadelphia: University of Pennsylvania Press, 1961.

Stephens, J. M., *Educational psychology: the study of educational growth*. New York: Holt, Rinehart and Winston, Inc., 1951.

White, R. W., Motivation reconsidered: the concept of competence, *Psychol. Rev.*, 1959, *66*, 297–333.

4 | THE DIVISION OF LABOR BETWEEN HOME AND SCHOOL

In examining the traditional task of the school, we have suggested the existence of three types of mechanisms, each of which provides nurture for a certain range of tendencies. Maturation provides the major contribution for the most basic tendencies. Urgent parental concern develops as the contribution of maturation ceases to be adequate. And the spontaneous forces of schooling take over as the urgent concern of parents begins to diminish.

So far, we have treated each of these forces as though it were completely independent of the other two. Speaking technically, the curves in Figure 3.2 are treated as though each were a dependent variable of the immediacy of survival value. The behavior of each curve is determined by this immediacy of survival value and by nothing else. So far we have not suggested that the shape of one curve is in any way affected by the status of the others.

Our treatment so far can best be explained analogously. Suppose some central traffic authority had allocated specific sections of a highway to three separate police units. Each of these three units is told where to concentrate its men and where merely to provide some casual coverage. But in all this, the distribution of effort is determined strictly by geographic landmarks. No unit is to take note of what the adjacent units are doing.

Such a distribution of forces clearly provides for fairly complete coverage and for a division of labor which permits the use of specialized equipment at the most needed points. As seen in the forces responsible for the nurture of tendencies, the provision of three independent mechanisms would guarantee many of the survival needs.

But such a system of independent forces would permit dangerous gaps. To provide fairly complete coverage, some of the mechanisms must be able to respond to the status of the others. As the patrols of one division are withdrawn from a boundary zone, the other division must be prepared to cover the gap. As maturation fails to provide the necessary nurture for breathing or swallowing, the urgent concern of parents must rush in to make good the deficit. As the urgent concern of parents is withdrawn to leave a vital area uncovered, some other agency should be able to respond to this neglect and provide the needed care.

Some of the direct linkage between one mechanism and another could come from spontaneous tendencies similar to those invoked to account for schooling. We could suggest, for instance, some blind, unthinking urges that impel us into action in the presence of worrisome deficit at whatever range of the survival gradient. For the most part, however, especially in dealing with sophisticated societies, we must more and more invoke deliberate human decision to account for some of the machinery whereby one mechanism is induced to rise as the influence of another mechanism becomes less and less adequate. In stressing the importance of nondeliberative forces, we hope we have in no way implied that rational deliberation has no survival value at all. Surely such deliberation has tremendous survival value. With complete consistency we can hold that deliberate rational decisions, although not considered as the chief or exclusive explanatory principles, must be accorded some part in determining the division of labor between the home and the school.

The classical *residual* theory of education (Peters, 1932), assumed that the work of the schools was entirely determined by the areas neglected by the home and by other primitive agencies. According to this theory the school *ought* to do "whatever needs to be done but which no other agency is adequately doing. It begins where other agencies leave off" (p. 254). By and large, moreover, this is not only what the schools are obligated to do, but it is also, for the most part, what they actually have done.

This more intimate relation between the concerns of the home and the work of the schools is suggested in Figure 4.1. In this figure, the ordinate represents the amount of attention that the school gives to any specific tendency or trait. The base line indicates the remoteness or indulgence of parental concern. The arbitrary traits placed along the base line are supposed to represent differences in the type of parental concern. At the left we find traits for which the home shows a concern that is immediate, urgent, and continuous. As we move toward the right, we find traits for which the home still feels some concern, but a concern that is increasingly remote, indulgent, and sporadic.

It should be clear that the curve in Figure 4.1 is by no means presented as an *explanation* of the school's concentration of effort. Since we have

Figure 4.1. The school's emphasis on traits in relation to the remoteness of parental concern for those traits.

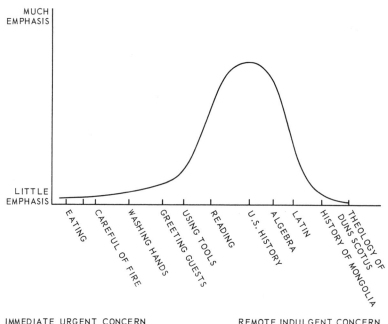

already defined (Chapter 3) the concept of "schoolness" as something that excludes the immediate parents, we must expect to find that the school concentrates on tasks neglected, in some way, by parents. Figure 4.1 merely attempts to give a more precise picture of the emphasis of the school and tries to emphasize the key role of *urgency* of parental interest.

The division of labor, demanded by the very concept of schooling, is found in many cultures. In Mead's (1943) classical parallels, the immediate parents provide the emphasis on industry. They take responsibility for the traits immediately necessary for survival. The areas less vital to survival are left to older siblings or to grandparents. The child nurse provides salutary play, and the grandparents provide the important, but less vital, mastery of legend and tribal lore. The Hopi father (Henry, 1955) takes on himself the responsibility for teaching his sons how to make a living but leaves to uncles and other ceremonial parents the responsibility of preparing the sons for rituals and initiations.

The Division of Labor as Affected by Rational Considerations

As we have already mentioned, it would be wrong to suggest that rational decisions are the only factors that cause the work of the school to be linked to the nature of parental concern. Parents may not know, for instance, why they ignore spelling, and the school may be equally unaware of its reasons for taking this subject under its wing. In many instances, however, deliberate, rational considerations may play a part, and these should be explored.

At times it may be a feeling of incompetence that leads parents to ignore some important subjects. In such matters as piano playing, for instance, parents may feel a frequent and urgent concern. They may restrain the expression of this concern, however, because they fear meddling in such a specialized subject. Some feeling of incompetence may come from ignorance of the subject matter. The typical parent, for instance, is in no position to give expression of interest in such things as Spanish grammar, histology, or aerial navigation. Parents may have no knowledge of the details of these subjects and therefore would have no means of detecting an error if one should appear. Even if they should suspect an error, they might hesitate to express themselves for fear of being wrong.

In addition to lack of mastery of subject matter, the home may feel a lack of competence in instructional ability. The typical parent may feel that the adequate mastery of golf or of automobile driving calls for an elaborate and intricate instructional procedure which is beyond his powers. Consequently, even though parents feel competent to pass judgment on the adequacy of any specific performance, they may decide that the entire responsibility should be transferred to someone who is an expert in the instructional matters.

Deliberate decisions on the part of school people probably played a part in the systematic shift in the school's effort that characterized progressive education (Cremin, 1961). In that phenomenon we saw the schools refusing to concentrate exclusively on the typical academic subjects and extending their influence to the "real life" curriculum heretofore left to the home or other agencies.

This shift in the school's emphasis may have been a deliberate response to areas that increasingly were neglected by the home as living conditions changed. The correct use of tools, for instance, was once a matter of immediate, inevitable concern to parents. Later, however, even the most conscientious parent would have little opportunity to express his underlying concern for this topic. Some parental neglect may have come from the outright selfish abdication of irksome responsibilities. The home has frequently been charged with such neglect in the areas of character, courtesy, civic responsibility, and in the development of taste. Whatever the basis for parental neglect, the school, sensing the neglect of important areas, may have conscientiously and deliberately shouldered the additional responsibilities.

In deliberately deciding to take care of the more vital areas, the school people may have been moved by some considerations that were far from lofty, although quite understandable. To some extent this may have come from the schoolman's uneasiness over his reputed preoccupation with academic matters, such a preoccupation being regarded as somewhat unwholesome. Many school people may have resisted the implication that their chief responsibility lies in the field of these useless, or luxury activities, and may eagerly have sought some correction.

The gradual shift to the left may also be due to some kind of empire-building on the part of school people. This tendency to extend one's domain to include as much territory as possible is very prevalent in many human enterprises, and there is no reason to suppose that school people are wholly exempt from it. Presumably this natural tendency is enhanced by the practical rewards to be gained from a larger enterprise. At any rate, it is quite possible that many teachers and administrators have been anxious to take over as much control as possible and bring a larger and larger area into the domain of formal schooling.

Any urge toward aggrandizement would not, of course, explain why the school might tend to drop the subjects to the right of the gradient. On the contrary, if the drive were merely to extend control, the school would be expected to retain the more academic matters while reaching out for more and more territory to the left. Consequently, the urge for power cannot be the only reason for this shift.

In this discussion we are concerned with understanding the mechanisms of schooling and not with the problem of making practical recommendations. Nevertheless at a later point (Chapter 9) we shall consider some of the issues involved in the possible shift in the school's ancient responsibilities. At that time we shall ask what should happen if the urgent concern of the home shrinks farther and farther to the left. Should the school also move to the left and spread its interest over the unblanketed area? Should some new, less scholastic agency be established to act as the community substitute for parental concern? If the school takes on responsibility for the vital traits in the middle gradient, will it lose its effectiveness to the right? If the present school is redeployed to guard the middle gradient, will the surviving societies of the future be those who have evolved or stumbled upon some new custodians of the "useless" traits to the right?

Effect of Cultural Innovations

It might be held that sheer technical advances or cultural innovations will alter the curriculum of the school. The increasing place of science in the school's curriculum, for instance, may be due not to any shift in interest but to the sheer fact that this subject became available for study. According to the view adopted here, however, the mere emergence of new material is not bound to affect the curriculum. It will do so only if that new material occupies an appropriate place on the gradient. Some of the problems presented by cultural or technological changes may have immediate significance in the home, and these may never reach the school. Television programs may present problems which the home cannot overlook, and these may be faced within the home itself. Other problems presented by the innovations may evoke only remote interest and thus become candidates for a place in the school. The new ideas concerning soil conservation, for instance, if they elicited some remote concern in the home, may well find a place in the school's activities.

It is most likely that all these forces have been acting in some degree. Circumstances must have removed many aspects of behavior from the direct scrutiny of the home. The home may be less zealous in cultivating many of the traits which do come to its attention, and, as we have seen, either or both of these circumstances would call for an extension of the school's influence. It is quite possible, moreover, that the school may be actively seeking more influence, partly in rebellion against its traditional and restricted role and partly in a natural urge to extend its influence.

REFERENCES

Cremin, L. A., *The transformation of the school: progressivism in American education, 1876–1957*. New York: Knopf, 1961.
Henry, J., Culture, education and communication theory, in G. D. Spindler, ed., *Education and anthropology*. Stanford, Calif.: Stanford University Press, 1955, 188–213.
Mead, Margaret, Our educational emphasis in primitive perspective, *Amer. J. Sociol.*, 1943, *48*, 633–639.
Peters, C. C., *Foundations of educational sociology*. New York: Macmillan, 1932.

5 | SCHOLASTIC ATTAINMENT: The Role of Background Factors

In a very general and schematic fashion we have tried to show how in strict theory the postulated spontaneous tendencies might account for the existence of the schools and for the nature of the tasks upon which the schools have concentrated. This has been a prelude, of course, to the more serious enterprise of showing how these same spontaneous tendencies can explain the work the school actually accomplishes. Before attempting this new task, however, we should consider some general background factors that may also play a part in the mastery of academic tasks. These are the forces on which the spontaneous tendencies must build or with which they must interact.

Maturation

Whenever a young child is subjected to instruction, several things may be happening. Obviously, he may be learning. He may also be growing old enough to profit from the instruction. The presence of these two forces makes it difficult to know just how much has been accomplished by the program of instruction. We see clearly, for instance, that, after six years of instruction, the twelve-year old can read much better than he could six years ago. But does this improvement come entirely from the six years of instruction? Probably not. During this time, the pupil was also increasing in his ability to learn. If we had waited until this ability had developed, he might have acquired all this mastery in one or two years.

In general, the literature points to the fact that, in the case of young children, a given amount of instruction is more effective when applied to an older child than when applied to a younger child (Baer, 1958; Hall, 1963; Tyler, 1964). Much of the change that takes place during the period of instruction can properly be attributed to this salutary maturation.

In stressing the fact that maturation often plays a part in academic growth and that it often contributes to this growth, we are merely trying to explain some general facts of schooling. We are in no sense recommending what the school ought to do about these general maturational trends. Certainly we do not wish to imply that, whenever possible, instruction should be deferred. There are many exceptions to our general rule. In some areas we could wait too long. On occasion, furthermore, we would be justified in ignoring the theoretical advantages from deferred instruction.

These practical problems, not relevant to our problem of explaining the process of schooling, are treated sketchily in a postscript to this chapter. Meanwhile, at this point, we merely make the claim that, very often, much of what is accomplished during the period of schooling may come not from the actual instruction but from the sheer fact that, during this period, the child is becoming old enough to learn.

Out-of-School Agencies

The school is not the only agency that acts on the child while he is acquiring the maturity necessary for learning. During his maturing years he is continually confronted by academic materials in his experiences outside the school. Parental chitchat assails him with concepts and factual information. Picture magazines, books, and billboards project letters and words at him. The ubiquitous television confronts him with words portraying the glories of various cosmetics while the voice of the model provides the auditory counterpart of the printed symbols.

It is not surprising that children learn a good deal about academic matters apart from the school. Many first graders, about to be exposed to formal schooling, already know many geographic facts such as the names of some oceans. They may also know that Russia is a country, and one we would do well not to forget (Huck, 1955). Grade-three children, just about to undertake formal instruction in social studies for the first time, already know about one third of the materials prepared for their education (Kaltsounis, 1964).

It is to be expected that out-of-school agencies would accomplish more in the areas of social studies and current affairs than in the more technical fields such as reading or spelling. This common-sense expectation, it will be noted, is also in line with the residual theory of schooling and with the postulates of the theory of spontaneous schooling.

All in all, in an attempt to account for the academic attainment that takes place within a school, we can never forget the contributions made by the home and the general community. To estimate the general academic performance that will occur in a given school, ask first about the general intellectual level of the children and the social and economic background of the parents (Kemp, 1955). This information will account for almost sixty percent of all the differences that will be found from school to school. After that, inquire about the *general* forces within the school—the general morale, about the interest and zest of the teachers, and about their reputation for learning and for teaching. This information will account for an additional six percent of the differences between one school and another.

The differences that are to be attributed to intellect and home background, of course, become evident only after some degree of schooling. If the pupil had never been to school at all, the differences in academic attainment would be less pronounced since the scores would be bunched close to zero. Provide this modicum of academic stimulation, however, and the variations in the resulting achievement will be seen to be linked largely with nonscholastic forces.

The Reputation of the School

We now have a maturing child already exposed to many quasi-academic experiences apart from the school. At this point, our child approaches the school, prepared to experience its formal program of instruction. But before he enters these new doors, the child has already been influenced by the school. To some extent he must be aware of the school as an institution concerned about academic matters. Just as churches are places where one foregoes boisterous play and thinks religious thoughts, so schools are places where it behooves one to have an eye to his academic manners (Stephens, 1933). The school is a place where one cannot take liberties with grammar, spelling, and with mathematics.

There is, then, a general force that arises from the school's reputed concern for academic matters. This force, coming from the school's reputation, persists throughout the child's goings and comings to and from school. In a similar way, during his stay at the outdoor camp, our older student comes alive to one set of cues. On the street corner he is more alert to different stimuli. In the school still other cues and stimuli take on a significance they would lack if they occurred in any other setting. Even in other settings these same academic matters will take on additional significance because the school, by its sheer reputation, has called attention to their importance.

At this stage we have a child acquiring the ability to learn and growing up in an environment containing thousands of different stimuli. Through their sheer existence and through their reputation, the schools have, to some extent, convinced him that "these aspects of the environment (words, symbols) are important." By this sheer process of directing his attention to the importance of a certain area, we have begun some instruction or have laid the basis for it.

General Sanctions Supplied by the School

Many sanctions are at work before the teacher begins to instruct. As soon as the teacher does begin to instruct, moreover, one of his first contributions is to add to the general sanctions already in operation. In the very process of conveying information about a given topic, the teacher also says, by implication at least, "This information is important." In the act of demanding one answer rather than another, he again says, in effect, "It is important how you deal with these matters." These forces are at work even when the teacher conveys very little precise information or fails to distinguish clearly between acceptable and unacceptable answers.

To see how these sanctions work, even when no information is being conveyed, let us consider an experiment in which the class is ostensibly learning the location of certain key cities in the United States. The pupils know that they are supposed to be learning this material. The teacher flashes the name of a city on the screen. A few seconds later he flashes the name of the state in which the city is to be found. It happens, however, that the projector is out of focus and the images are so blurred that the pupils cannot decipher them. Under these circumstances the pupils would acquire no information, nor would they be able to determine whether or not they had thought of the right state. But they could not fail to be impressed with the fact that cities do have a state location, and somebody thinks this is important.

Some aspects of this hypothetical illustration were actually employed by Entwisle (1961) in an attempt to test the influence of sanctions, or of set, or enhancement of stimuli. As in the hypothetical illustration, the children were supposed to be learning the states in which certain key cities were located. In the aspect of the study dealt with here, moreover, the projector was also used, but the focus was quite clear.

One group of children was tested on the state locations of some fifty-eight cities. The children in this group were then given three separate lessons on the locations of *half* of these cities. The lessons were distributed over a period of two months. During the times that these pupils were assembled for instruction, a control group was also assembled but spent the time reading in the library.

Compared to the control group, the instructed group did show a significant gain on the cities that they had studied during the training sessions. But, again compared to the control group, they also made a significant gain on the similar items that *they had never studied.* As might be expected, however, the gain on the unstudied items was less than the gain on the items presented during the practice periods.

By the sheer act of calling attention to a certain class of items and by implying that pupils should know such items, the school can induce some growth. To bring about this growth, one would have to make sure that the pupils encountered the items in question. In the experiment just cited, the material was of the type that pupils would probably come across in their out-of-school experience. For more esoteric items it would be necessary to go to some trouble to arrange for the necessary encounters.

After some growth is induced by the very general sanctions supplied by the school, additional growth is produced by specific instruction. The pupils who actually receive instruction will ordinarily be found to learn more than those who are merely led to believe that the material is important. But the latter do learn something. Not all the observed growth can be attributed to the detailed processes of instruction.

The Combined Effects
of Background Factors

Professor Courtis (1949) reports some data which highlight the important role of these general background factors. In one school system, grade-eight children were taught to spell the word "sincerely." The word "customary" was not taught at all. Children were tested on both of these words from grade two through grade nine. Each year there was a steady increase in the number of children able to spell both words, even before "sincerely" was taught. In grade eight the mastery of "sincerely" spurted ahead, suggesting the role of specific instruction. Mastery of "customary" continued to increase at the regular rate through grades eight and nine. By grade nine the advantage for "sincerely" had dropped off, and the mastery of the two words was indistinguishable. Throughout the period from grade two to grade nine there was a marked increase for both words.

Except, then, for a short period of specific instruction, the pupils learned the words at about the same rate. During the seven-year period, be it noted, mastery of both words was facilitated by the pronounced increase in general maturity. Both words were probably encountered in out-of-school experiences and in casual experiences within the school. Because of its reputation and because of the general expression of its concerns, the school had given the impression that "spelling is important." This force applied to both words. Because of all these general background factors, both words were increasingly mastered as the children grew older. When specific instruction was applied to one of them, there was a slight and transient advantage for the word being taught.

These are the background factors that we must keep in mind when we turn our attention to the impact of the teacher's meaningful instruction. The experience induced by the teacher does not fall upon an inert object. It falls instead on a maturing organism, sensitized by the school's reputation and by the school's general concerns, and already exposed to many academic subjects encountered outside the school's walls.

REFERENCES

Baer, C. J., The school progress of underage and overage students, *J. educ. Psychol.*, 1958, *49*, 17–19.

Courtis, S. A., The rate of growth makes a difference, *Phi Delta Kappan*, 1949, *30*, 316–323.

Entwisle, Doris R., Attensity: factors of specific set in school learning, *Harv. educ. Rev.*, 1961, *31*, 84–101.

Hall, C. V., Does entrance age affect achievement?, *Elem. Sch. J.*, 1963, *63*, 391–396.

Huck, Charlotte, Children learn from their culture, *Educ. Leadership*, 1955, *13*, 171–175.

Kaltsounis, T., A study concerning third graders' knowledge of social studies content prior to instruction, *J. educ. Res.*, 1964, *57*, 345–349.

Kemp, L. C. D., Environmental and other characteristics determining attainment in primary schools, *Brit. J. educ. Psychol.*, 1955, *25*, 67–77.

Stephens, J. M., *The influence of the school on the individual*. Ann Arbor, Mich.: Edwards Bros., 1933.

Tyler, F. T., Issues related to readiness to learn, *Yearb. Nat. Soc. Stud. Educ.*, 1964, *63*, Part I, 210–239.

INCIDENTAL COMMENT: Some Practical Problems in Exploiting the Advantages of Deferred Practice

In trying to make sense out of educational data, we may well assume that maturation ordinarily facilitates instruction, and the longer we wait, the greater the result to be gained from a given unit of instruction. In making practical decisions, on the other hand, there are many considerations that lead us to question this rule.

In the first place, whatever the truth of the general principle, there are important exceptions. Maturation does not always work to the advantage of learning. At times we can wait too long. True enough, it is useless to expose a child to a certain kind of experience when he completely lacks the physical and mental structures necessary for dealing with that experience (Flavell, 1963). By the same token it may be dangerous to withhold that experience or to provide inadequate experience after the structures have begun to develop. According to the theories of Hebb (1949) and Piaget (Flavell, 1963; Hunt, 1961) and from the evidence on imprinting and sensitization (Hess, 1959; Moltz, 1960), we must face the possibility that there is a golden period during which the organism can deal effectively with a given experience. If he is denied this experience at the proper time, the underlying physical or mental structures may never develop properly, and the inadequate adaptations may be impossible to correct. During the school years, moreover, there may be a similar disadvantage from waiting too long if the child is to learn to speak a foreign language without an accent (Stern, 1964) or if he is to become proficient in acrobatic dancing.

So far we have asked whether we should supply experience at an early age or withhold it. Obviously, however, we do not always have this choice. The child may get some experience in a given subject even if we fail to supply it. And this inadvertent experience may lead him to learn the wrong things. Under these circumstances it might be better to give him the proper experience, even at a less efficient stage, than to face the necessity of unteaching the errors he would otherwise acquire. There is evidence, for instance, that some concepts in science can be more readily mastered in grade nine than in grade ten (Yager and Dessel, 1962). There are also reports that eighth grade pupils may exceed comparable pupils in grade nine in the mastery of algebra (Friesen, 1962; Lawson, 1962). These more recent studies, it is true, go against the trend of the earlier evidence. Some of the upset may come from the well-known Hawthorne effect and from the enthusiasm of the younger pupils from being allowed to tackle topics ordinarily reserved for their elders. It is also possible that the older pupils were handicapped by interfering things they had already learned.

There are other, more cogent, reasons for hesitating to transform the school system in order to take advantage of the fact that learning is typically more efficient at a later age. True enough, it will take less effort to teach a child of ten to learn to read than to teach the same skill to a child of six. But think of the rich experience denied the child between the ages of six and ten! *As far as the child is concerned,* moreover, the saving of time or the increase of efficiency is not a very important consideration. Suppose, for instance, it will take the six-year old three hours to master what the ten-year old could learn in one. What will the six-year old do with these two hours we have saved him? In view of the many competing interests that press upon the ten-year old, one hour for him may be more costly than three hours for the six-year old.

Finally, there is always the danger that a child who has learned to get along without reading during the years from six to ten may feel less need for this skill when we do ask him to acquire it.

REFERENCES

Flavell, J. H., *The developmental psychology of Jean Piaget.* Princeton, N.J.: Van Nostrand, 1963.

Friesen, E. J., A comparative study of the achievement of eighth- and ninth-grade algebra pupils in the Wichita intermediate schools, *Bull. Nat. Ass. Sec. Sch. Prin.*, 1962, *46*, No. 271, 370–371.

Hebb, D. O., *The organization of behavior*. New York: Wiley, 1949.

Hess, E. H., Imprinting, *Science*, 1959, *130*, 133–141.

Hunt, J. McV., *Intelligence and experience*. New York: Ronald, 1961.

Lawson, F. R., A comparative study of the achievement of eighth- and ninth-grade students in beginning algebra (1961), *Bull. Nat. Ass. Sec. Sch. Prin.*, 1962, *46*, (No. 271), 372–373.

Moltz, H., Imprinting: empirical basis and theoretical significance, *Psychol. Bull.*, 1960, *57*, 291–314.

Stern, H. H., Curriculum research and the introduction of a foreign language into the primary school, *Educ. Res.*, 1964, *6*, 86–103.

Yager, R. E., and N. F. Dessel, Ninth versus tenth grade placement of general biology, *Sci. Educ.*, 1962, *46*, 436–439.

6 | SPONTANEOUS TENDENCIES AND SCHOLASTIC ATTAINMENT

The maturing child is now in the presence of the teacher. He is already sensitized to the school's demands and has already met some of those demands by virtue of his nonscholastic experience. He is also equipped with the machinery through which he may learn whenever that machinery is adequately engaged by some suitable forces. We must now look for some forces, emanating from the teacher, by means of which those mechanisms of learning may be brought into play.

In many discussions of teaching, it is taken for granted that the forces of instruction are closely geared to the deliberate intention of the teacher. Hughes (1963), for instance, cites four definitions of teaching recently put forward (p. 26). All four definitions stress the teacher's intention, and in some of these, intention is the crucial factor. Smith (1961) holds that so long as the teacher intends to induce learning his actions shall be called teaching, whether or not any learning is accomplished. Even when the effectiveness of the teacher is taken into account, some writers would look only at the accomplishment of the *intended effects*. According to Medley and Mitzel (1963) the "competence of a teacher is defined as the average success of all his behaviors in achieving their intended effects" (p. 81). Eisner (1964) maintains that *"All* teaching introduces into a situation a set of conditions intended to influence the behavior of the pupils" (p. 118, italics added).

It will be no surprise to learn that the treatment proposed here will not rely exclusively on the deliberate, intentional acts of the teacher. These deliberate acts are considered as rather late additions, or refinements, imposed on more primitive, spontaneous forces that would operate quite apart from deliberate intentions or in defiance of unnatural intentions.

The spontaneous tendencies to be invoked are, of course, no strangers. They are the same tendencies that were tentatively proposed (Chapter 3) in very general fashion to account for the evolution of the school as a social institution. These same tendencies are now seriously put forth in detail to account for the work that is accomplished in the schools. There is an intriguing parsimony in the thought that the same forces which may have led to the very existence of the schools should also serve as the crucial factors in furthering the detailed work that goes on in the schools. As the school comes into existence, from whatever causes, the spontaneous tendencies would accomplish a good deal even in the complete absence of deliberate decisions.

The spontaneous tendencies postulated in Chapter 3 are as follows:

Spontaneous manipulative tendencies

1. The cluster of playful, manipulative tendencies, which lead many people to stress matters that have little immediate payoff and which other people treat indulgently.

   These manipulative tendencies are supplemented by several clusters of spontaneous *communicative* tendencies.

Spontaneous communicative tendencies

2. Spontaneous tendencies to talk of what we know.
3. Spontaneous tendencies to applaud or commend some performances and to disapprove or correct other performances.
4. Spontaneous tendencies to supply an answer which eludes someone else.
5. Spontaneous tendencies to point the moral.

These forces, let loose within the existing school, would, in and of themselves, induce a substantial measure of educational attainment even in the absence of rational, deliberate decisions, in the absence, indeed, of any intent to teach.

Teaching in the Absence of Deliberate Intention

To see how these tendencies would operate in the absence of a deliberate intention to teach, let us imagine some adult who is unusually well endowed with the specified spontaneous tendencies. This adult, that is to say, has more than average interest in some subject which has little immediate payoff and which other people acknowledge to be worth knowing although they give it only casual or occasional attention. Let us suppose, for instance, that this man is a Lincoln buff, and he is greatly preoccupied with Lincolniana and Lincoln anecdotes of all kinds. To complete his armament of spontaneous tendencies, we will have to suppose that, to an unusual extent, our adult is impelled to talk to any convenient listener about Lincoln and Lincoln matters. More than most people, moreover, he also finds it hard to restrain himself when he finds others making erroneous statements about Lincoln. He also, quite automatically, shows pleasure or comments approvingly when other people speak of Lincoln in a way that satisfies him. Whenever anyone else is speaking of Lincoln and stops to grope for a word, or a date, or a name, our adult is also impelled to supply the correct item. When an opportunity presents itself, he is compelled to point the moral.

Having selected our adult as one somewhat above average in the prescribed spontaneous tendencies, we must now make sure that he maintains sustained contact with a group of maturing children. In Chapter 3, it will be remembered, we suggested that such an adult would automatically direct his attention to children and would thus spontaneously initiate a school. But at the moment we are concerned with the way in which these tendencies operate after the adult is already within a school setting. To bring him into this setting, without suggesting that he is supposed to teach, let us tell him that, in the schedule of a certain group of ten-year olds, one period per day has not been provided for. We prevail on him to baby-sit with these pupils for forty minutes per day until we can find a regular teacher. We assure him that no subject of instruction has as yet been assigned to this period, and he will not be expected to teach. We ask only that he hand over the class and the classroom in reasonably intact condition to the teacher who takes over at the end of the period.

This seemingly unnatural situation, artificially contrived to illustrate a theory, is not without its fleshy counterparts. Teachers have been known to hold class without feeling responsible for any given subject. Mark Harris (1959), for instance, is alleged to have claimed: "I don't teach subjects. I teach what I am thinking about, and we read what I am reading at the moment. The main thing is to make it interesting for yourself." In a second journalistic mention, Mr. Harrison Tweed, the lawyer, is being interviewed on schools he has supported. In speaking of a summer camp he had once organized, Mr. Tweed comments as follows: "George Luks, the painter, was my best faculty member."

"What did Luks teach?" we asked.

"He didn't teach anything," said Mr. Tweed. "He just talked. He was out there to enjoy himself. He made a lasting impression on the boys." (Talk of the Town, 1959)

The Mechanisms of Learning to Be Engaged

If the postulated spontaneous tendencies are to induce educational achievement, they must in some way engage the mechanisms of learning that are to be found within the child. We must now look briefly at these mechanisms of learning and see how the spontaneous tendencies might link up with the mechanisms in some effective way.

Unfortunately, as it happens, there is some disagreement about the various mechanisms of learning (Hilgard, 1964; Hill, 1963). For this reason, the mechanisms to be presented are somewhat general and, even so, must be hedged by a number of qualifications to make them acceptable to one theorist or another.

Motivation   Although psychologists do not agree completely either on the nature of motivation or on its role in learning (Hilgard, 1963; Leeper, 1963), there are a few conditions that can be listed with some confidence. It is possible that, provided other conditions are appropriate, motivation does little or nothing in and of itself to bring about learning. According to this view, the chief purpose of motivation is (a) to get the student into the situation in which learning can occur, (b) to keep him at a reasonable level of activation, (c) to direct his attention to one feature of the environment rather than another, and finally, (d) to elicit from him those acts or responses which he must make if learning is to occur.

Practice or Experience   If a pupil is to learn some material he certainly must have some experience with the material; often he must have a great deal of experience. The amount of experience necessary is a matter of controversy. According to one view (Rock, 1957), the process of learning is similar to the process of shaking a coin out of a piggy bank. With luck, one shake will be sufficient. If the first trial fails, however, other shakes will be necessary. These later shakes do not push the same coin farther through the slot. They merely provide further opportunities for a favorable outcome.

The theory of single-trial learning is in great dispute (Lockhead, 1961), however, and many theorists think that practice exerts its effects by successively increasing the same force, as when we drive a nail farther into the plank by successive applications of similar blows.

Intriguing Subsequent Events The more vigorous current theories of learning, without exception, hold that the pupil's act or behavior should be followed by some moderately noteworthy event. When the child has answered correctly he should see the teacher smile or hear him say, "Good." When the rat has reached a certain point in the maze he must encounter something that engages his interests, or something that has some impact upon him, or that distracts his attention from the circumstances that have been acting on him thus far.

According to the *reinforcement* theorists, this subsequent event, especially if it is beneficent, acts directly to confirm the behavior that has just occurred. By one process or another this reinforcement strengthens the association or connection responsible for the behavior. Some theorists (Skinner, 1953) refuse to go beyond this general claim. Others, Hull and his followers (see Hill, 1963), for instance, hold that this intriguing event must reduce some effective need or distress (hunger, pain) currently acting on the organism, or it must act as a surrogate for the relief of some distressful condition in the past. Still others hold that this intriguing event serves to provide a focus around which the experience can be organized. It thus becomes a basis for insight. To some psychologists, this intriguing event merely separates the episode that has just occurred from the experience that is to follow (Hill, 1963). But for one purpose or another, most theorists claim that some such event (or reinforcement) must occur.

Insight or Cognition Formation It has been noted that, for some psychologists, the chief function of the intriguing event that follows behavior is to permit the formation of a clear-cut structure (Miller, Galanter, and Pribram, 1960; Tolman, 1951). When the door that is stuck finally yields, providing an intriguing sequel to our struggle, the learner forms the idea that "doing 'this' leads to the opening of the door." This idea, or *cognition*, proves to be useful in subsequent encounters with the recalcitrant door. This valuable structure, or cognition, or *insight*, is more likely to occur when the subsequent event is interesting, or meaningful, or when it is brought forcefully to our attention.

Substitution or Guidance According to the late E. R. Guthrie (1952), the great goal in all learning is to get the learner to perform a given act while he is being influenced by certain conditions. If you want the child to learn to say "dog" whenever he encounters the letters *dog,* your great problem is to make sure that, on one occasion, he will say "dog" while the letters are part of his experience. It is easy enough to be sure that the letters are part of his experience. But now you must get him to say "dog." There are many ways to do this. You see him hesitating, for instance, while he confronts the strange symbols *dog*. At this point, you yourself need merely say, "dog." He will often echo your remark and at this moment you have him saying "dog" while the letters are acting on him. Now all you have to do is to quit while you are ahead, so to speak. To do this you introduce some intriguing new stimulus like "good" or "wonderful," so that the association just acquired will be insulated from the experience to follow.

The Power of the Spontaneous Tendencies to Engage the Mechanisms of Learning

We now return to the Lincoln enthusiast who is liberally endowed with the spontaneous tendencies but who lacks any intention to teach. To what extent can we expect that these spontaneous tendencies will engage the various mechanisms considered to play a part in learning?

Granted an adult who bubbles over continuously regarding Lincoln and his doings, we can be sure that a child regularly associating with that adult will be in a place where he can learn about Lincoln. He will also have his attention directed toward facts in the life of Lincoln. We cannot be so sure that the student's level of activation will be high. Depending on the teacher and the circumstances, the pupils may sit entranced, empathizing with every facet of the experience being portrayed. They may be somewhat listless, or they may be found in some intermediate state of activation. But, in this connection, we must remember that few theories of learning demand a high level of activation throughout. Such interest and zest is an attractive experience in its own right, but it is not always essential for learning. For some learning, activation should be kept at quite moderate levels.

Even under the most ordinary circumstances, pupils associating with our adult should get the idea that someone thinks Lincoln is important. We cannot be sure just how much they will be impressed by this fact. If the adult is a person whom the pupils take seriously, if he carries a measure of prestige, then his concern for Lincoln may also be taken quite seriously. If he strikes the pupils as being a nonentity, his idiosyncratic interests may be regarded as trivial or laughable. But by and large, Lincoln matters should take on some additional importance through his expressions of concern.

Two kinds of practice or experience can be expected, one almost inevitable and the other highly probable. A pupil listening to a story about Lincoln, and doing nothing more than listening, is still engaging in a very important kind of activity or practice. The listener seldom, if ever, follows the speaker word by word. Often he trails behind. Frequently, however, he outruns the speaker and anticipates the words that are about to come. The tendency to anticipate what is to come is so prevalent that it can be used as a measure of intelligibility of reading materials (Rubenstein and Aborn, 1958). If the listener does not make any correct anticipations we can be sure that he is getting very little out of the material being read. If he can anticipate too much, of course, the material is conveying very little new information and may be boring. But some anticipation is highly probable and is most salutary. As we shall see later, such anticipation permits the application of reinforcement.

This moment-by-moment activity that goes on while reading (or listening) is not to be scorned. From it a great deal of achievement or mastery may result.

Along with this silent activity going on in the minds of all listeners, some pupils may react overtly by asking questions, offering comments, or raising objections. At times our adult may spontaneously ask questions, rhetorical or otherwise, and his questions may elicit overt answers.

A measure of relevant reinforcement seems inevitable. In the first place, there is unavoidable reinforcement when a listener anticipates the words of the speaker. If the listener anticipates correctly, then the actual words of the speaker, when they do appear, will confirm this anticipation and provide a most acceptable kind of reinforcement. If the anticipation should prove to be incorrect, this reinforcement will be lacking and the underlying tendency should become weaker.

For the overt statements or questions of the pupil, reinforcement or intriguing subsequent events are also inevitable, provided our adult is endowed with the prescribed spontaneous tendencies. By definition, such an adult would be bound to commend or approve a statement that he regarded as correct. He would be bound to reject or correct a statement or comment that he regarded as inappropriate.

In all this we should not disregard the many minor grimaces or automatic reactions displayed by our spontaneous adult. Without trying, without even knowing what he is doing, he looks incredulous, or bewildered, or surprised when he encounters a statement that does not fit his standards. Conversely, his face shows pleasure or relief as the pupil's statements begin to hit home or fit in with the adult's idea of what is right. These subtle automatic expressions of approval or disapproval, as the overt expressions discussed above, do not need to be cultivated. On the contrary, they are extremely difficult to suppress. We must work hard to retain a poker face when someone is taking liberties with our specialty. Even then, the more discerning can detect slight expressions of dismay when the provocations become extreme.

These automatic or nondeliberative reinforcements are by no means confined to the chance adult who lacks the intention to teach. They probably play an enormous role in the everyday work of the "intentional" teacher. For every time that any teacher marks a question right or wrong or administers an overt expression of approval or disapproval, there are scores of occasions when his face shows a look of surprise, bafflement, incredulity, patient waiting, or relieved acceptance. These subtle grimaces, these shadows and lights, these nuances in tone of voice, are in play day in and day out as the teacher faces the class. They are very effective reinforcements. They come and go with very little deliberate rationale on the part of the teacher. And yet, it is quite possible that they contribute enormously to educational growth.

For some theorists, the great factor in learning is to attain an insight or an awareness of what leads to what. From his experience with the material being learned, the pupil gets the idea that "turning the handle this way leads to the opening of the door" or "pumping the accelerator too often leads to flooding the engine." Some of these insights arise with no help from other people. Often, however, the insight can be sharpened by the comments of an astute observer. To acquire a well-structured insight, the pupil must see that it is this *particular behavior* that leads to that *specific result*. In this task he may have difficulty either in getting a clear view of the *behavior* in question or in seeing exactly what *result* was produced. The adult observer will often help in both tasks. In the first place he can show just what behavior leads to the result in question. He can say, "This punishment (result) is not for breaking the dish (behavior A) but for lying about it (behavior B)." It is behavior B and not behavior A that leads to the result. "It was your triumphant gloating (behavior A), not your actual winning the game (behavior B), that made George sulk." "The thing that makes me so happy (result) is you not only did well in the play (behavior A), but you were also able to help Susan when she was in trouble (behavior B)" (A combination of A and B gets the result.)

In the second place, the observer can often call attention to a result that may elude the learner. The mother says, "See! The cat stops swishing his tail when you stroke him that way." "See how much more time we have when you get dressed before you turn on the television."

This urge to point the moral is often quite spontaneous. It acts on many people as a sort of compulsion, even when social taboos or hearer resentment warn them away from such unasked comments. Our Lincoln fan, strongly equipped with this urge, could hardly help pointing out, "It's because you overlook Lincoln's concern for national unity that you see any weakness in his antislavery stand." "See how much clearer things become when you take his early legal experience into account."

Guidance or substitution is also bound to be used by one liberally supplied with the spontaneous tendencies. In this process of guidance we merely direct or maneuver the student toward the right answer while the question, or task, or problem is still acting on him or is still part of his experience. As he struggles to recall the name of Lincoln's mother, we supply the answer for him. When this happens, he frequently repeats or echoes the answer we supply and is thus led to make the correct response while the question is acting on him.

This tendency to guide the speaker into the answer that eludes him is so prevalent that many cultures have erected taboos against it. Many sophisticated teachers, moreover, go to some trouble to hold it in check. For the adult having no conception of himself as a teacher, however, this tendency would operate quite freely.

The frequent taboos and the sophisticated teacher's self-imposed restraint suggest that this device can be overworked. And this is true. To the extent that the pupil is guided into the answer by the teacher's comment, he may not get the full benefit of the reinforcement that normally follows. Reinforcement may be most effective when it follows an unaided response emitted by the pupil. It may be of less value when it follows a response that the pupil merely parrots after the teacher. But, to say that this device can be overworked or that it is not self-sufficient is not to say it is useless. During the early stages in mastering a given task, this prompting or supplying of the answer can be of great help.

Along with the prompting or guidance that is overtly supplied by the spontaneous tendencies of our adult, there is an additional supply of guidance at work in the sheer process of listening. In anticipating what is about to come, we may hit the mark and thus experience reinforcement as the speaker confirms our guess. But we may be in error. The teacher's completed remarks then fails to supply reinforcement but, by the same token, it does supply guidance and points out the anticipation we should have made. Our adult, for instance, remarks, "Since Lincoln was born in . . . ," and at this point he has to stop to clear his throat. During the brief interval one listener silently thinks, "Kentucky," a second listener silently thinks, "Illinois," whereas a third finds his mind a blank. The adult recovers his voice and continues, ". . . Kentucky." This word, now uttered, provides substantial reinforcement for the first listener. For the second listener it fails to provide reinforcement but does guide him into the response that he should have made. The third listener gets similar guidance. It is not unusual, as a matter of fact, for such corrected listeners to make some such silent comment as, "Of course. 'Kentucky.' That is what I should have said." "I was just going to say that."

The General Impact of the Spontaneous Tendencies

It seems inevitable that our adult, completely innocent of any intention to teach, would be forced to engage the various mechanisms necessary for learning and would bring about a considerable attainment in the subject of his interests. There is, indeed, something quite comforting in the thought of these tireless forces contained in the automatic concerns and compulsions of even the least sophisticated of teachers. No lesson plan is needed to invoke the expression of these interests. The spontaneous expressions of dismay or delight come to the "teacher's" countenance with no effort or no conscious awareness on his part. This is most fortunate. The total effort would be intolerable if each of these grimaces and changes in expression had to be controlled by a deliberate decision.

It must be pointed out, however, that not everyone is so enamored of these unthinking tendencies to which the teacher gives spontaneous expression. Wallen and Travers (1963), for instance, admit that much of the teacher's activity springs from his own inner needs and not from his rational decisions. The urge to talk is one such need they cite. But these authors hold that, in giving vent to this need, as when he lectures to his students, the teacher is doing harm (p. 461). They do not see in the spontaneous expression of such needs the basic mechanisms of instruction. Other theorists, however, take a more indulgent attitude toward the teacher's urge to hold forth (Smith, 1963).

The Coordination of the Tendencies and Mechanisms

Whenever we find a mechanism of learning we also seem to find some spontaneous tendency that stands ready to engage that mechanism. At first glance, this may sound all too pat. Our credulity may be strained by this very compact arrangement. Actually, however, it is not at all mysterious that these two phenomena should be so aptly geared together. The learning mechanisms and the tendencies that engage them probably evolved hand in hand. The complex machinery involved in reinforcement, we must remember, would confer little benefit on the race unless there were some aspect of the environment capable of setting that machinery in motion.

The advantage from some linkage is also seen when we turn to the powerful spontaneous tendencies, allegedly responsible for schooling, that we have acquired during our long evolutionary journey. These tendencies would not serve their postulated survival function if they failed to link up, in some effective way, with the mechanisms that produce learning.

All in all, then, in pointing out the manner in which the tendencies and the mechanisms interact, we are in no way dealing with a suspiciously convenient coincidence. On the contrary, we merely note a grim, survival necessity.

The Effect
of a Sense of Mission

Clearly, in portraying an adult completely devoid of any intention to instruct, we have had to develop a rarity if not a fiction. It is unlikely that many such missionless adults would be found in the classroom. Most adults in such a situation would assign themselves some mission, and the mission most likely to be thus self-assigned is surely that of instruction.

This sense of mission, obviously, is not an integral part of the theory of spontaneous schooling. It is an additional beneficent force that is imposed upon the more primitive spontaneous tendencies. Such a sense of mission, however, could affect the operation of the more basic forces, and, consequently, it should be taken into account.

The sense of mission is a dimension in its own right. At one extreme of this dimension we might find the teacher who grudgingly admits that he is expected to develop some skill or accomplishment in his pupils. At the other extreme we find our true evangelist, frantically eager that everyone shall partake of the glories of his subject. In between these extremes we can find any degree of intention to teach. To a certain extent this sense of mission can be induced. It can be induced by the mere announcement that teaching is expected. It can also be developed as an obligation in exchange for salary. Clearly this phenomenon of a sense of mission should be studied. We should inquire into the forces, noble and mundane, that lead people to go to some trouble and to make considerable sacrifice in order to carry the message to more and more people.

Whenever this sense of mission is present, it should have some bearing on the operation of the spontaneous tendencies. For one thing this sense of mission, induced or built-in, could serve to some degree as a substitute for the spontaneous tendencies. An adult might be markedly deficient in the spontaneous urges that ordinarily lead people to cherish offbeat matters and to talk about the matters they cherish. He could still take on the chore of teaching, however, merely for pay or from a sense of duty. Having no strong spontaneous interest in nature study, for instance, and being only moderately well equipped with the urge to speak of any interests he does have, our synthetic teacher could still hold forth on the doings of birds in the same way that television announcers force themselves to expound on the glories of some new deodorant.

On the basis of our theory we would expect such a person to work under difficulties. Unless he could come to affect the spontaneous interests that he lacks, he would have to rely on a series of deliberate acts to accomplish what is painlessly and gladly performed by a person suffused with the spontaneous urges.

A sense of mission should also affect the teacher who is already fairly well endowed with the spontaneous tendencies. Concern for the pupil's status is a case in point. In describing our spontaneous, missionless adult, it will be noted, we never indicated that he knew or cared how much the pupils knew about his subject. He would be sad if *no one* could converse with him about his subject. He is distressed when *anyone* mistreats his subject. But he is never constrained to ask, "Just how far has Martha Brown progressed in this area?" The teacher having a genuine sense of mission, however, must, by definition, feel some concern about that status of his pupils. This concern and the knowledge that it brings might well affect the process of instruction.

A sense of mission also implies a conscious concern for objectives (see Chapter 12). The spontaneous, missionless adult may be innocent of any goals or objectives and may be similarly ignorant and indifferent about what he is doing to the children. The dedicated, deliberate teacher, on the other hand, must have some goals and must have some objectives in mind. Such goals and objectives should lead to a more *business-like* and systematic approach (Ryans, 1960). The missionless but "spontaneous" teacher, on the other hand, could go about things in a quite disorganized fashion.

In some of the modifications it produces, a strong sense of mission could impede the free operation of the primitive, spontaneous tendencies and could, in this way, interfere with instruction. For the most part, however, one would expect that in acquiring a sense of mission or in augmenting the mission he already has, the teacher would make more effective and systematic use of the forces that would be available to him without that mission.

But however much he may add to them, the teacher never relinquishes the spontaneous forces. These blind, automatic tendencies are inevitably at work when even the most sophisticated teacher deliberately sets out to instruct. Underlying his deliberate intention, these automatic, spontaneous tendencies inevitably bring about motivation, practice, reinforcement, guidance, and the enhancement of insight. This statement, of course, is no real disparagement of the deliberate efforts that are added to the primitive forces. In the same way, it is no real disparagement of the physician to emphasize the many automatic mechanisms that are at work, before he applies his deliberate efforts, which may also contribute to recovery along with his elaborate therapy. In both his case and in ours, such forces, if they exist, should not be fearfully disowned but should be sought out, investigated, and, if justified by further study, used as the basic pattern of forces on which our deliberate efforts might be imposed.

REFERENCES

Eisner, E. W., Instruction, teaching, and learning: An attempt at differentiation, *Elem. Sch. J.*, 1964, *65*, 115–119.

Guthrie, E. R., The psychology of learning, rev. ed. New York: Harper & Row, 1952.

Harris, Mark (Journalist's report), *Saturday Rev.*, July 18, 1959, *42*, No. 29, p. 17.

Hilgard, E. R., ed., Theories of learning and instruction, *Yearb. Nat. Soc. Stud. Educ.*, 1964, *63*, Part I.

Hilgard, E. R., Motivation in learning theory, in S. Koch, ed., *Psychology: a study of a science*, Vol. V. New York: McGraw-Hill, 1963, 253–283.

Hill, W. F., *Learning: a survey of psychological interpretations.* San Francisco Calif.: Chandler, 1963.

Hughes, Marie M., Utah study of the assessment of teaching, in A. A. Bellack, ed., *Theory and research in teaching.* New York: Teachers College, Columbia University, 1963.

Leeper, R. W., Learning and the fields of perception, motivation, and personality, in S. Koch, ed., *Psychology: a study of a science*, Vol. V. New York: McGraw-Hill, 1963, 365–487.

Lockhead, G. R., A re-evaluation of evidence on one-trial associative learning, *Amer. J. Psychol.*, 1961, *74*, 590–595.

Medley, D. M., and H. E. Mitzel, The scientific study of teacher behavior, in A. A. Bellack, ed., *Theory and research in teaching.* New York: Teachers College, Columbia University, 1963, 79–90.

Miller, G. A., E. Galanter, and K. H. Pribram, *Plans and structure of behavior.* New York: Holt, Rinehart and Winston, Inc., 1960.

Rock, I., The role of repetition in associative learning, *Amer. J. Psychol.*, 1957, *70*, 186–193.

Rubenstein, H., and M. Aborn, Learning, prediction, and readability, *J. appl. Psychol.*, 1958, *42*, 28–32.

Ryans, D. G., *Characteristics of teachers.* Washington, D.C.: American Council on Education, 1960.

Skinner, B. F., *Science and human behavior.* New York: Macmillan, 1953.

Smith, B. O., Toward a theory of teaching, in A. A. Bellack, ed., *Theory and research in teaching.* New York: Teachers College, Columbia University, 1963, 1–10.

Smith, B. O., A concept of teaching, in B. O. Smith and R. H. Ennis, eds., *Language and concepts in education.* Skokie, Ill.: Rand McNally, 1961, 86–101.

Talk of the Town, Educator, *New Yorker,* August 22, 1959, *35,* No. 27, p. 25.

Tolman, E. C., *Collected papers in psychology.* Berkeley, Calif.: University of California Press, 1951.

Wallen, N. E., and R. M. W. Travers, An analysis and investigation of teaching methods, in N. Gage, ed., *Handbook of research on teaching.* Skokie, Ill.: Rand McNally, 1963, 448–505.

7 | THE CONSTANCY
OF THE SCHOOL'S
ACCOMPLISHMENT

Some years ago Wilson (1958) compared the achievement of grade-three pupils in two different cities. The schools in these two cities did not differ in the amount of time devoted to reading, spelling, or arithmetic. The pupils examined, moreover, were of comparable general ability. In administrative "advantages," however, the two cities differed markedly. In one city, all children had had the benefits of kindergarten education. In this city, the classes were also kept down to an average of thirty pupils each, and all teachers had received four years of training. In the other city, in contrast, none of the children had been to kindergarten, the classes averaged thirty-eight pupils, and the teachers had received only two years of training. When the pupils were compared on tests of arithmetic, spelling, and reading, there was no advantage whatever for the city with superior facilities. And differences that did appear regularly favored the city with larger classes, with the shorter period of teacher training, and with no kindergarten.

Wilson's study brings together a number of paradoxical results. But such results are by no means novel. For many years, as a matter of fact, scholars have noted a vast preponderance of such negative results. Within educational circles, this preponderance has been treated as a matter of common knowledge, calling for no documentation. A quarter of a century ago, for instance, Peters and Van Voorhis (1940, p. 476) state quite simply that the vast majority of educational experiments reveal differences which are not statistically significant. Almost two decades later, Nachman and Opochinsky (1958) make a similar comment and feel no need to supply evidence to support their remarks.

To say that many scholars comment on the impressive trend of negative results is not to say that the commentators necessarily accept this trend at its face value. More often than not, the commentator merely notes the trend and then goes on to show why it is misleading.

But no matter whether this trend of negative results will be viewed as common knowledge or as a surprising revelation, it should be brought together and given some documentary warrant. A complete documentation, as it happens, would be extremely unwieldy. The relevant studies run into the thousands, and, even then, no one could be sure of complete coverage. To keep the documentation within workable limits, I rely, wherever possible, on the conclusions of those who have summarized a number of investigations. When the summaries are very old, individual studies of more recent date are also added. The first summary to be reported is an ancient compilation of my own. The others, being put together by quite a variety of people, should be less contaminated by the specific biases or preconceived notions that I may bring to the task.

General Summaries

The early summary by the present writer (Stephens, 1933) included some two hundred investigations dealing with a variety of administrative factors. This survey reported only a slight relation between attendance and achievement. School cost and achievement were also unrelated when measurements were based on comparable pupils. In many investigations, but not all, size of school had little, if any, influence on attainment. Over two score investigations were unanimous in finding that pupils in large classes learned as much as their colleagues in small classes. A few investigations suggested that students who were prepared in "accredited" high schools got along no better in college than comparable students who were prepared in high schools which did not meet the accreditation standards. A sampling of the many experiments on methods of teaching revealed very little advantage for any one method. The methods which stressed visual aids or individual instruction seemed to have a slight but irregular advantage. Between the other methods, however, there was little to choose. One method was about as good as the other and no better.

A survey by Harris (1940), based on college performance, confirms the trend reported in 1933. Harris reports that attendance at a large high school or at an "accredited" high school is no dependable passport to success in college, and class size is immaterial. Harris failed to find any clear-cut advantages for any of the following procedures: sectioning students according to ability in language classes; giving weekly quizzes to motivate learning; replacing one class period by a program of independent reading; or substituting discussion or other methods of instruction for the lecture method.

During the early 1940s, Eaton and his associates (Eaton, 1942, 1944; Smith and Eaton, 1945) studied the general trends in achievement-test results of Indiana schools. These were based on mass tabulations involving 10,000 or 15,000 pupils and hundreds of schools. The results consist of raw trends with no attempt to hold any other factors constant when the influence of one factor is being considered.

According to these studies, achievement seemed to be unaffected by size of class, size of school, amount of time given to instruction, or by the administrative organization of the schools. In some of the reports, the length of the school year appeared to be related to achievement, but in other reports it was not.

Later general reviews of research on administrative factors (Ellis, 1960; Hatch and Bennet, 1960; Herrick, 1960) similarly report failure of such research to show a definite advantage for any one approach over another.

Summaries of Studies on Specific Administrative Factors

In presenting the conclusions based on the many summaries that are available, we include an occasional interpretative comment when it seems especially in order. For the most part, however, the interpretations are deferred to a later section.

Attendance   Summarizing the bulk of the evidence on attendance, accumulated during the first half of the century, Heck (1950) reports as follows: "While research at the moment is not conclusive, what there is tends to refute the too common assumption that absence results in a harmful effect upon scholarship as expressed by marks" (p. 920).

This conclusion clearly agrees with earlier summaries (Finch and Nemzek, 1940). When intelligence is held constant, the correlation between attendance and achievement clusters between .10 and .20, with occasional correlations reaching a value of .30.

Television   To what extent does the pupil's achievement come from the detailed, managed interaction between pupil and teacher? Does achievement fall off if the teacher becomes less able to adjust his deliberate efforts to each pupil's mastery of the subject?

The teacher on the television screen is completely oblivious to the status of each student in the subject being taught. Nor can this mechanical teacher modify his efforts to suit the varying needs of the pupil. Yet, from some hundreds of experiments (Schramm, 1962), we can detect no clear difference between the results achieved by instructional television and those from other procedures. Of the 393 investigations, 255 reported no significant difference. Of the remainder, 83 favored television, and 55 showed an advantage for the regular classroom. A later summary by Barrington (1965) covered some 30 investigations and revealed the same equivalence for television and classroom instruction. Schramm suggests that for the young children there is a slight benefit from instruction by television, and for college students there might be a slight handicap. But in no case can the difference be large, even if it exists at all.

In these experiments, of course, there are several factors at work. The television instructor can go to great trouble to prepare his lesson and can use close-up views and other materials not ordinarily available to the regular instructor. Perhaps these advantages cancel out the handicap arising from lack of individual attention.

But the solution cannot rest entirely in these additional facets that television can bring to instruction. Even when students listen to nothing more than a tape recording of a lecture, their achievement is no less than that of students listening to the lecture itself (Popham, 1962).

Independent Study and Correspondence Courses   In an early review of the efficacy of correspondence study at the college level, Bittner and Mallory (1933) found correspondence students somewhat ahead of students in the classroom. In a later review, Childs (1952) extends this same conclusion to secondary school pupils. Childs based this conclusion on eight separate experiments. Not all the reports favor the correspondence students, but the trend is clearly in that direction. The difference is very slight in any case and certainly cannot be interpreted as showing any definite advantage for the students in the classroom. The conclusions from these earlier reviews are borne out by isolated, later investigations (Childs, 1954; Dysinger and Bridgman, 1957; Parsons, 1957).

Correspondence-school students are formally committed to a course of instruction but lack some features of the typical pupil-teacher interaction. In the same way, students taking a course by independent study are formally committed to the course but lack the classroom contact.

When such independent study is elected on a voluntary basis, the students working on their own do just as well as those electing class attendance (Jensen, 1954; Milton, 1962).

With such self-selection of work, of course, it is always possible that it is the serious and motivated student who prefers independent work. This greater motivation, or interest, or seriousness of purpose, by the way, could also account for the fact that people lacking formal high school training frequently equal the typical high school students in college performance (Bent, 1946) or in performance on an objective test of General Educational Development (Leton, 1957).

In one investigation (Marr and others, 1960) the possibility of self-selection was eliminated. In this experiment students were arbitrarily assigned to one procedure or the other, and those assigned to receive one lecture per week excelled those not receiving the lecture. It would seem, then, that when interest and determination are held constant, class attendance will provide some additional help.

Size of Class   When teaching a small class, a teacher clearly comes to know more about the individual pupils in his charge (McKenna, 1957). But do pupils learn more from this increased attention on the part of the teacher? As indicated in earlier statements, this problem has been investigated as frequently as any in the entire educational literature (Fleming, 1959; Kidd, 1952; Powell, 1964). From several scores of investigations, the consensus is overwhelming. At all levels above the first few grades and in almost all subjects, the size of the class seems completely unrelated to the achievement of the pupils. If there is any advantage, it is in favor of large classes. Recent separate studies (De Cecco, 1964; Marklund, 1963; Eash and Bennett, 1964) confirm this historical consensus. Marklund, for instance, made some 281 separate, but not wholly independent, comparisons and found that 37 comparisons favored the large classes, and 22 favored the smaller class, whereas 222 showed no significant difference. Even in a subject such as fundamentals of speech, where one would ordinarily expect an advantage for smaller classes, there appears to be no loss when some of the instruction is given by mass lecture (Giffin and Bowers, 1962).

Against this overwhelming mass of negative results, some exceptions are to be noted. Powell (1964) mentions three studies, from the scores conducted, that seem to find an advantage for smaller classes. It is true, moreover, that students tend to prefer smaller classes (De Cecco, 1964). There are isolated reports that college students may give an instructor a more favorable rating when they encounter him in a small class (Powell, 1964). But this is by no means the prevailing trend of the most substantial investigations (Riley and others, 1950).

Individual Consultations   From earlier reports there was some evidence (reviewed by Hoehn and Saltz, 1956) that performance improves when each student is interviewed at length (thirty to sixty minutes) by a trained psychologist with a clinical bent. In their own investigation, Hoehn and Saltz arranged for individual conferences between students and instructors. The latter were not psychologists but regular classroom teachers who were given a brief orientation on how to interview. From a variety of approaches and from various amounts of interviewing, the investigators could find no difference in the performance of students interviewed and those not interviewed.

The consultations discussed so far have been one-shot affairs. As an extension of this sort of consultation, there is the tutorial system in which the student meets regularly with his instructor for discussion and guided reading. The results of the investigations in this area are in conflict. One early investigation (Greene, 1934) reported that such guided reading produced results superior to either a straight lecture course or a program of independent study. In a study conducted about the same time, Hartmann (1935) arranged that half the students should attend class three hours per week, whereas the other half should attend twice a week and spend the third hour in individual consultation with the instructor. The latter students fell behind the others. A later study (McKeachie and others, 1960) also found that students relying on extensive tutorial help fell behind those assigned to a conventional class.

Counseling   Students doing poorly in classwork are often referred to a specialized counselor for intensive help. The early investigations made use of students voluntarily seeking such help and, for this reason, it was difficult to eliminate the factor of motivation. Later investigators, however, have typically made sure that the counseling is applied to a random sample drawn from a pool of volunteers. In reviewing four such studies, Callis (1963) reports that two of them found no difference in the achievement of the counseled and uncounseled students. One reported an advantage for the counseled students, and one reported mixed results. Of two well controlled studies appearing too late for Callis' review, one (Shouksmith and Taylor, 1964) found an advantage for the counseled students, and one (Winborn and Schmidt, 1962) found that the students not counseled made a superior gain.

Instead of receiving individual counseling, students may be assigned to classes in "how to study." Here again, the evidence varies, but by and large such courses seem to help in student achievement (Entwisle, 1960).

Deliberate Intent to Influence   In a direct attempt to manipulate the intensity of the teacher's efforts, Tilton (1947) first selected thirty-seven pupils out of the total enrollment in six fourth-grade classes. He then asked the six teachers involved to concentrate especially on the three or four students selected by the experimenter from that teacher's class. The teacher was asked specifically to try to increase the performance of these pupils in arithmetic. The net effect was zero. Of the thirty-seven pupils selected, ten did show more gain than the pupils not selected. But some fell below the average gain, and the overall performance of the selected pupils was on a par with those not selected.

What happens when we try to increase the intensity of the educational forces by enlisting the aid of the home? From a group of high school students doing poorly in school (Schoenhard, 1958), some 158 were assigned to a home-visitation group, and 158 comparable students served as a control. Teachers visited the homes of the selected students and arranged for a series of follow-ups by telephone, letters, and consultations with students. In each of four grades, the two groups were compared at the end of four different intervals. Of these sixteen comparisons, ten favored the control, and six favored the home-visitation group. Only four of the differences were significant, however, and of these, two favored the home-visitation, and two favored the control.

Increasing the Student's Involvement   Along with our attempts to increase the amount of contact between teacher and pupil, we could employ devices to increase the student's application to his task. We could get him to become more involved in his subject, to study longer or harder or to avoid distractions.

Students learning by television may be tempted to adopt an extremely passive attitude and may be inclined to act as mere spectators. To overcome the possible disadvantages of this attitude, one group of investigators (Jacobs and others, 1963) encouraged the pupils in some fifteen fifth-grade classes to take an extremely active part. The students were asked direct questions about the television program. They were also urged to make written responses and to bring in illustrative material. These pupils achieved no more than comparable students not so stimulated. To a greater extent than the controls, the stimulated pupils came to dislike television instruction.

In contrast to these results, Gropper and Lumsdaine (1962) found superior performance on the part of students making active responses, provided the lesson itself was carefully programmed. When the responses were made to a regular unprogrammed lesson, no such advantage appeared.

Amount of Time Spent in Study   In an early summary, Strang (1937) reported six investigations showing almost no correlation between achievement and time spent in study. Here we face the possibility that dull students may study more and achieve less, and this factor might mask the advantage of increased study. This earlier summary is borne out by a more recent study at the college level (Jex and Merril, 1959). In contrast to these results, however, Ryans (1939) had found correlations of .20 to .40 between achievement on a brief assignment and time spent in study for that particular assignment.

Distraction   In general the influence of apparent distractions is almost negligible. College students earning money learn about as much as those not so distracted (Newman and Mooney, 1940; Trueblood, 1957). College students perform just as well when they engage freely in extracurricular activity as when these activities are curtailed (Brambaugh and Maddox, 1936; Remmers, 1940). Younger pupils spending much time with television or radio do about as well in school as those of comparable intelligence who give little time to such entertainment (Heisler, 1948; Ricciuti, 1951; Thompson, 1964).

Size of School   In many general discussions, the small high school has been rather sweepingly condemned and its abolition recommended. Along with the general discussion there have been many investigations designed chiefly to see if a student's success in college is in any way affected by the size of the high school from which he comes. Although the research has received less publicity than the general discussions, a substantial body of data has been available for some time. In one of the pioneer compilations, Douglass (1931) summarized seven earlier studies and reported on one of his own. He concluded as follows: "In spite of the fact that all studies seem to show that in the smaller high schools will be found less experienced, more poorly trained, more poorly paid, and more heavily loaded teachers, inferior housing and equipment, more restricted curricular offerings, less well developed programs of guidance and counseling and other less desirable conditions, graduates of small schools should not be discriminated against as applicants for college entrance. Their achievement in college is in no material degree inferior to that of graduates from larger schools" (p. 57).

Some eighteen years later Garrett (1949) summarized another six studies and in these found no evidence for a relation between high school size and college achievement.

Ten years after Garrett's summary, Hoyt (1959) extended the summary to seventeen investigations and added one of his own. Of the seventeen earlier studies, five found no advantage for either large or small schools. The advantage lay with the large schools in six studies, with the smaller schools in three, and with medium sized schools in three.

Hoyt's own study reported no significant difference in achievement between schools of different sizes.

The studies reported in these reviews vary in the extent to which they have controlled such factors as intelligence and home background. Most of them have made some efforts in this direction. Off hand, one would expect that failure to control such factors should lead to a spurious positive relation, since, by and large, background factors tend to be more favorable in the larger communities in which the larger schools are more likely to be found. In one recent study, (Street and others, 1962) we do find a positive relation between school size and attainment when intelligence and background factors are not taken into account. Conversely, Lathrop (1960), arranging for a meticulous control of both intelligence and type of high school program followed, found no relation between size of high school and college success. Studies attempting to control both intelligence and broad social background report mixed results. Kemp (1955) earlier noted an effect from school size, but Wiseman (1964) failed to duplicate this result.

In this discussion, of course, the emphasis has been upon academic achievement. The development of the "whole child" may be another matter, and in this area Barker and Gump (1964) suggest many advantages for the small high school.

Selection and Training of Teachers Among the scores of studies dealing with teacher effectiveness, there are quite a few that try to relate the characteristics of the teacher to the achievement of the pupils being taught. To an overwhelming extent the results are negative. True, there is some suggestion that experience helps for a few years, but after those early years the older teacher is less effective (Ryans, 1960). In contrast to this suggestion of positive results, however, we find almost no relation between the academic gains of pupils and the qualities of the teacher that can be observed by principals or supervisors. Medley and Mitzel (1963), for instance, cite results from eight specific studies and refer in general terms to many others. They conclude that, "a reading of these studies reveals uniformly negative results" (p. 257).

Easing the Teacher's Load Before the days of the modern ungraded classroom, the presence of two classes in a single room was considered an evil. Clearly such a mixed assignment seemed to impose more of a burden on the teacher and seemed to dilute the attention the teacher could give to any one class. The studies, however, have shown no harmful effect (Adams, 1953; Knight, 1938; Stephens and Lichtenstein, 1947). These studies were conducted before the ungraded school had been advocated. It is too soon to give any confident assessment of the ungraded school itself, but there is some evidence (Hopkins and others, 1965) that it is about as effective as the traditional procedures, but no better.

Offhand, one would suspect that team teaching would reduce the load for any given teacher. This is also a relatively recent innovation (Shaplin and Olds, 1964), and it is too soon to judge its effectiveness. The studies (Ginther and Shrayer, 1962; White, 1964; Zweibelson and others, 1965) emerging so far, however, suggest little, if any, consistent difference between the effectiveness of team teaching and the more traditional approaches. Lambert and his associates (1965) found team teaching to be somewhat less effective. In the Zweibelson report (1965), however, we find a favorable student attitude toward team teaching.

Ability Grouping   Homogeneous grouping should also permit the teacher to concentrate his efforts on a narrower range of problems. Ekstrom (1961) reviewed some thirty investigations on the effectiveness of homogeneous grouping. She found no identifiable advantage or disadvantage for the procedure. In a later review, Pattinson (1963) reported a similar lack of difference. An extensive series of experiments from Stockholm (Marklund, 1963; Svensson, 1962) and one from Utah (Borg, 1965) confirm this suggestion of comparable attainment under heterogeneous and homogeneous grouping.

Differences in Policy or General Approach   The violent argument about progressivism in the schools (Cremin, 1961) led to a variety of predictions and claims. On the one hand, we find "the critics" holding that progressivism would soon spell disaster for the schools, if it had not already done so. On the other hand, we note the innovators themselves suggesting that marked advantages should follow from the new approaches. Inevitably this has led to a flood of "then and now" studies in which the achievement of pupils at any one time is compared with performance in the schools of more recent date (Boss, 1940a, 1940b; Caldwell and Courtis, 1924; Gerberich, 1952; Gray, 1952; Harding, 1951; Leonard and Eurich, 1942; Muir, 1961; Wrightstone, 1951).

The many studies reported in these treatments vary tremendously in scope, in care, and certainly in outcome. The most frequent claim of the more comprehensive reviews is that of insignificant, or inconsequential, or inconsistent differences. A slight advantage for the older schools in one study seems promptly offset by an equally slight advantage for the modern schools appearing in another study. The great claim of the proponents of modern education is the progressive school *has held its own* in the matter of the three R's, and it has done this in spite of its concentration on a wider, real-life curriculum.

The outstanding result of the famous eight-year study (Chamberlin and others, 1942) is the rough academic equivalence of pupils from traditional and from progressive schools. In a careful analysis of this classical study and of ten other studies dealing with the same problem, Wallen and Travers (1963) report as follows: "In summary, the findings indicate no important differences in terms of subject matter mastery and a superiority of the progressive students in terms of the characteristics which the 'progressive school' seeks to develop" (p. 474). Here again, we find that there is at least no academic loss to be incurred when some of the school's attention is directed to real-life concerns.

The excitement and hopes once associated with the progressive movement have now been transferred to the new curriculums, especially to those in science and mathematics. So far we have only spotty evidence about the effectiveness of these innovations on which so much effort has been expended. The trends, however, both from the occasional summary (Brown and Abel, 1966; Burns and Dessart, 1966) and from isolated studies (Rainey, 1964; Lisonbee and Fullerton, 1964), again foreshadow the ancient refrain of no significant differences. Here again we detect the same bright spot: The new procedures result in no loss to the traditional material and may also induce some growth in topics not touched by the traditional curriculum.

Discussion versus Lecture   To many people it seems obvious that the discussion method should surpass the lecture. Yet summary after summary (see Stovall, 1958) can find no warrant for the assumption. Citing some sixteen studies, Wallen and Travers (1963) comment as follows: "With respect to immediate mastery of factual information, most studies find no significant differences between lecture and discussion methods" (p. 481). Along with this preponderance of negative results, they report four studies showing an advantage for the lecture and one favoring the discussion method. The matter of retention, as opposed to immediate mastery, has been investigated less frequently. Two studies of retention favor the discussion method, and one favors the lecture method.

McKeachie (1963), in a review of college teaching, also stresses the rough equivalence of lecture methods and discussion methods in inducing knowledge of subject matter. McKeachie does point out, however, that courses using a problem-solving, discussion approach may excel the lecture courses in producing skill in problem solving. The trends developed by these recent summaries are in line with those appearing earlier (Stovall, 1958).

Group-Centered versus Teacher-Centered   A discussion method need not be group centered, although many discussions do emphasize the goals and purposes of the class. The effect of this group-centered approach has been treated in a number of summaries (Anderson, 1959; Sears and Hilgard, 1964; Stern, 1963). Here again we find practically no differences in achievement. There may be a slight preponderance in favor of the teacher-centered methods, but the difference is very slight and by no means consistent.

Use of Frequent Quizzes   At the college level, students receiving frequent quizzes during the term learn about as much as those receiving only one midterm quiz, but they learn no more. This equivalence appeared in Noll's (1939) early summary of investigations and is borne out by recent isolated studies (Selakovitch, 1962; Standlee and Popham, 1960).

Programmed Instruction   It is too soon to sum up the evidence on programmed instruction. In the flood of reports (Lumsdaine, 1964) now appearing, however, there is much to suggest that this device is about on a par with other methods of individual study (Poppleton and Austwick, 1964; Owen and others, 1965). It may permit an average saving of time over straight classroom approaches, but its overall superiority to classroom teaching is by no means apparent (Feldhusen, 1963; Feldman, 1965).

Interpreting the Negative Results

Almost anyone familiar with the general literature will admit the vast number of negative results in the data from experiments. Not everyone, however, will agree on the interpretations. A great many rival hypotheses have been advanced, many of them suggesting that we should not take these results at their face value.

One Narrow Segment of Achievement   As one *ad hoc* explanation of negative results, it is pointed out that the experiments test only one narrow segment of achievement, namely those academic aspects of growth which are easy to test. The argument goes on to say that great changes in other aspects of achievement, especially in personality or character, might be discerned if these were tested.

Insensitivity   A second argument contends that our tests are not only too narrow in their scope, but they are relatively insensitive even in the area in which they do function. This argument implies that more sensitive measures might detect considerable growth which now escapes observation.

Poorly Controlled Investigations In the flood of investigations lying behind the various summaries, we will find much variation in rigor and in scientific care. Many of the investigations clearly failed to control factors that could have affected the results.

Overcontrolled Investigations A fourth explanation attributes the lack of positive results not to lack of control but to "overcontrol." The educational investigator, in his zeal to become superscientific, has been held to control the investigation "to death," so to speak. In his effort to make sure that extraneous factors are held constant, he has held the whole growth process constant. It is often suggested, for instance, that the control of intelligence automatically restricts the differences that might be expected to appear in such a closely related thing as academic achievement. Consequently, it may often happen that a given pedagogical technique is really very superior, but it does not have enough freedom of movement to show itself.

Tests of Significance Peters and Van Voorhis (1940) contend that, in judging whether or not significant positive results exist, we have used a criterion that is much too strict. Often we have refused to admit that a difference is significant unless we can be guaranteed odds of 1 to 100 or 3 to 1000. In the face of a handicap such as this, it is no wonder that many results have been negative. It is a wonder that any have ever been positive.

There is much force in these arguments which seek to explain negative results as error or artifact. Each of the arguments briefly mentioned may turn out to have a considerable amount of truth. It is true that tests of wider aspects of growth may show the results of pedagogical innovations even when no difference appears in the narrower field of scholastic growth. It is true that more sensitive instruments may show marked differences where our present instruments draw a blank. It is true, also, that due to the many possibilities of subtle interaction, the restriction of any extraneous factor may also result in the restriction of the factor under observation. And it is true that we have held our experiments to most exacting standards.

But for all their claims to plausibility as partial explanations, we should not push these arguments too far. It is always possible that the vast number of investigations have "just happened" to hit on the more intransigent areas of growth. It is also possible that they have just happened to miss the areas which would have shown the effects of the device being tested. But these possibilites are not very comforting. The argument implies that some systematic force has been at work to keep our sample a biased sample. The argument rests on the assumption that the unmeasured areas of character growth are more responsive to the devices being tested than the more measurable areas of academic achievement. Actually that assumption is very dubious, a point which will be developed at some length in Chapter 9.

The other four arguments are all confronted by one very serious obstacle. The fact is, insensitive as the tests may be and overcontrolled or undercontrolled as some experiments probably are and exacting as the standards undoubtedly are, a great deal of growth does appear and does meet the standards. The investigations cited do not fail to reveal growth. They merely fail to reveal differences in growth attributable to the administrative variables. If we use other variables, such as background factors, moreover, marked differences in growth also come through. If the tests, and the designs, and the criteria of significance permit such differences to appear, it is difficult to see why they should not also permit differences in administrative factors to come through if these were present.

Inadequate Engagement of Basic Principles   In a more general explanation Wallen and Travers (1963) remind us that there are many forces (principles) at work to produce classroom achievement. These, they point out, have been imperfectly known. The experimenter, in groping in the dark, may so arrange his investigation that it happens to invoke one of these principles but fails to deal with the others. Even worse, a single innovation may engage one force so as to facilitate growth but may inadvertently act on another unknown force so as to inhibit growth.

Expectations from the Spontaneous Theory   The view put forward here is not unlike the suggestion of Wallen and Travers, with the exception that the spontaneous theory is intended primarily to explain what the school actually accomplishes. In providing a single, coherent theory to explain these positive accomplishments, we find the same theory automatically explains the flood of negative results as well. In considering the negative results, we merely have to remember the many forces that are at work to induce growth in almost any school situation. We should also remember that, in the typical comparison of two administrative devices, we have two groups which are comparable in the forces responsible for (say) 95 percent of the growth to be had and which differ only in the force that, at best, can affect only a small fraction of the growth.

The forces common to any two approaches are to be found both in the background factors (Chapter 5) and in the spontaneous tendencies (Chapter 6) that are always at work whenever the teacher is in the classroom. Suppose, for instance, that we are comparing two methods of teaching spelling to children in grade four. Through the forces of maturation, both groups are increasing in the ability to acquire skill in spelling. Both groups encounter spelling problems and opportunities in their experiences outside the school. Because of its reputation and the things it is known to stress, moreover, the school will further sensitize both groups to those spelling experiences encountered in the world at large.

As we turn to the different classrooms in which two different methods are being employed, we will still find much in common. In each class there is a teacher who knows how to spell and who spontaneously calls attention to matters pertaining to spelling. Both teachers are happy when the children spell correctly and are less happy when an error occurs. When the reason for the error can be formulated, each teacher spontaneously calls attention to this principle and to the results that follow when the principle is ignored.

With all these forces acting on both groups, we now arrange for some difference in the formal method of teaching. We cannot be sure, in the first place, that this difference in the formal approach will actually engage any of the basic primitive forces by which teaching is accomplished. But even if it does, this one slight change, imposed on the whole battery of powerful, prior forces, may have great difficulty in demonstrating its influence.

Our expectation of negative results is increased when we consider the very sequence in which different forces are applied. In a process such as educational growth, the first force to be applied is likely to have an unfair advantage. It can push the attainment of the children, through the easy portion of the curve of growth where a slight expenditure of energy brings about a considerable return in achievement. Each succeeding force that is applied must suffer an ever-increasing handicap. Administrative factors and pedagogical refinements, moreover, are notorious late-comers in this succession of forces. They are inevitably left to show their influence on that part of the curve where diminishing returns are the rule. In this part of the curve, the going is so heavy that a considerable effort will show only a limited increase in achievement, and a minor force will show nothing at all.

This impressive flood of negative results, although demanded by the spontaneous theory, cannot be used as proof of the theory. Negative results, however impressive, are notoriously unsatisfactory as proof of anything. What can we dependably conclude, for instance, from a sustained failure to observe a monster in Loch Ness? To explain such negative results, we can typically invoke the classical hypotheses of imprecision, excessive random error, and compensating interactions. We can also claim that we just did not try hard enough—that our doseages were inadequate, or our treatments were applied for too short a time. In the face of these inevitable rival hypotheses, any array of negative results could only be used to add to the plausibility of the theory. Failure to observe a pattern of negative results would have condemned it out of hand. That particular condemnation, of course, it has unquestionably escaped. But other and more telling tests are still to come.

REFERENCES

Adams, J. J., Achievement and social adjustment of pupils in combination classes enrolling pupils of more than one grade level, *J. educ. Res.*, 1953, *47*, 151–155.

Altman, Esther R., The effect of rank in class and size of high school on the academic achievement of Central Michigan College seniors class of 1957, *J. educ. Res.*, 1959, *52*, 307–309.

Anderson, R. C., Learning in discussion: A resumé of the authoritarian-democratic studies, *Harv. educ. Rev.*, 1959, *29*, 201–215.

Barker, R. G., and P. V. Gump, *Big school, small school: high school size and student behavior.* Stanford, Calif.: Stanford University Press, 1964.

Barrington, H., A survey of instructional television researches, *Educ. Res.*, 1965, *8*, 8–25.

Bent, R. K., Scholastic records of non-high school graduates entering the University of Arkansas, *J. educ. Res.*, 1946, *40*, 108–115.

Bittner, W. S., and H. F. Mallory, *University teaching by mail.* New York: Macmillan, 1933.

Bledsoe, J. C., An analysis of the relationship of size of high school to marks received by graduates in first year of college, *J. educ. Sociol.*, 1954, *27*, 414–418.

Borg, W. R., Ability grouping in the public schools, *J exp. Educ.*, 1965, *34*, No. 2 (whole issue), 1–97.

Boss, Mabel E., Arithmetic, then and now, *Sch. Soc.*, 1940a, *51*, 391–392.

Boss, Mabel E., Reading, then and now, *Sch. Soc.*, 1940b, *51*, 62–64.

Brown, K. S., and T. L. Abell, Research in the teaching of high school mathematics, *Math. Teach.*, 1966, *59*, 53–57.

Brumbaugh, A. J., and C. Maddox, Extra-curriculum activities: higher education, *Rev. educ. Res.*, 1936, *6*, 212–217.

Burns, P. C., and D. J. Dessart, A summary of investigations relating to mathematics in secondary education: 1964, *Sch. Sci. Math.*, 1966, *66*, 73–80.

Caldwell, O. W., and S. A. Courtis, *Then and now in education: 1845–1923.* New York: Harcourt, Brace & World, 1924.

Callis, R., Counseling, *Rev. educ. Res.*, 1963, *33*, 179–187.

Chamberlin, D., and others, *Did they succeed in college?* New York: Harper & Row, 1942.

Childs, G. B., A comparison of supervised correspondence study pupils and classroom pupils in achievement in school subjects, *J. educ. Res.*, 1954, *47*, 537–543.

Childs, G. B., Research concerning supervised correspondence study, *Bull. Nat. Ass. Sec.-Sch. Princ.*, 1952, *36*, No. 190, 7–29.

Cremin, L. A., *The transformation of the school: progressivism in American education, 1876–1957*. New York: Knopf, 1961.

De Cecco, J. P., Class size and co-ordinated instruction, *Brit. J. educ. Psychol.*, 1964, *34*, 65–74.

Douglass, H. R., The relation of high school preparation and certain other factors to academic success at the University of Oregon, *Univ. Oregon Publ. Educ. Series*, 1931, *3*, No. 1.

Dysinger, D. W., and C. S. Bridgman, Performance of correspondence-study students, *J. higher Educ.*, 1957, *28*, 387–388.

Eash, M. J., and C. M. Bennett, The effect of class size on achievement and attitudes, *Amer. educ. Res. J.*, 1964, *1*, 229–239.

Eaton, M. T., A survey of the achievement in social studies of 10,220 sixth-grade pupils in 464 schools in Indiana, *Bull. Sch. Educ. Indiana Univ.*, 1944, *20*, No. 3.

Eaton, M. T., A survey of the language arts achievement of sixth grade children in 18 counties and 6 cities in Indiana, *Res. Bull. Indiana Dep. publ. Instruct.*, 1942, No. 3.

Ekstrom, Ruth B., Experimental studies of homogeneous grouping: a critical review, *Sch. Rev.*, 1961, *69*, 216–226.

Ellis, J. R., The school program: general instructional procedures, *Rev. educ. Res.*, 1960, *30*, 49–56.

Entwisle, Doris R., Evaluations of study-skills courses: a review, *J. educ. Res.*, 1960, *53*, 243–251.

Feldhusen, J. F., Taps for teaching machines, *Phi Delta Kappan*, 1963, *44*, 265–267.

Feldman, Margaret E., Learning by programmed and text format at three levels of difficulty, *J. educ. Psychol.*, 1965, *56*, 133–139.

Finch, F. H., and C. L. Nemzek, Attendance and achievement in secondary school, *J. educ. Res.*, 1940, *34*, 119–126.

Fleming, Charlotte M., Class size as a variable in the teaching situation, *Educ. Res.*, 1959, *1*, 35–48.

Garrett, H. F., A review and interpretation of investigations of factors related to scholastic success in Colleges of Arts and Science and Teachers Colleges, *J. exp. Educ.*, 1949, *18*, 91–138.

Gerberich, J. R., The first of the three R's, *Phi Delta Kappan*, 1952, *33*, 345–349.

Giffin, Kim, and J. W. Bowers, An experimental study of the use of lectures to large groups of students in teaching the fundamentals of speech, *J. educ. Res.*, 1962, *55*, 383–385.

Ginther, J. R., and W. A. Shrayer, Team teaching in English and history at the eleventh grade level, *Sch. Rev.*, 1962, *70*, 303–313.

Gray, W. S., What is the evidence concerning reading? *Progressive Educ.*, 1952, *29*, 105–110.

Greene, E. B., Certain aspects of lecture, reading, and guided reading, *Sch. Soc.*, 1934, *39*, 619–624.

Gropper, G. L., and A. A. Lumsdaine, *Studies in televised instruction: The use of student response to improve televised instruction*. Pittsburgh, Pa.: American Institute of Research, 1962, pamphlet.

Harding, L. W., How well are the schools now teaching skills? *Progressive Educ.*, 1951, *29*, 7–14, 32.

Harris, D., Factors affecting college grades, a review of the literature, 1930–1937, *Psychol. Bull.*, 1940, *37*, 125–166.

Hartmann, G. W., Comparative pupil gains under individual conferences and classroom instruction, *J. educ. Psychol.*, 1935, *26*, 367–372.

Hatch, W. B., and Ann Bennet, Effectiveness in teaching, U.S. Office of Education, *New dimensions in higher education*, 1960, No. 2.

Heck, A. O., Pupil personnel work, II. School attendance, *Encyclopedia of educational research*. New York: Macmillan, 1950.

Heisler, Florence, A comparison between those elementary school children who attend moving pictures, read comic books, and listen to serial radio programs to an excess with those who indulge in these activities seldom or not at all, *J. educ. Res.*, 1948, *42*, 182–190.

Herrick, V. E., Administrative structure and processes in curriculum development, *Rev. educ. Res.*, 1960, *30*, 258–274.

Hoehn, A. J., and E. Saltz, Effect of teacher-student interviews on classroom achievement, *J. educ. Psychol.*, 1956, *47*, 424–435.

Hopkins, K. D., O. A. Oldridge, and M. Williamson, An empirical comparison of pupil achievement and other variables in graded and ungraded classes, *Amer. Educ. Res. J.*, 1965, *2*, 207–215.

Hoyt, D. P., Size of high school and college grades, *Person. Guid. J.*, 1959, *37*, 569–573.

Jacobs, J. N., J. H. Grate, and Ullainee M. Downing, Do methods make a difference in television education? *Elem. Sch. J.*, 1963, *63*, 248–254.

Jensen, B. T., Instruction and personality as factors in student performance, *J. educ. Res.*, 1954, *47*, 529–535.

Jex, F. B., and Reed M. Merril, Intellectual and personality characteristics of University of Utah students, *J. educ. Res.*, 1959, *53*, 118–120.

Kemp, L. C. D., Environmental and other characteristics determining attainment in primary schools, *Brit. J. educ. Psychol.*, 1955, *25*, 67–77.

Kidd, J. W., The question of class size, *J. higher Educ.*, 1952, *23*, 440–444.

Knight, E. E., A study of double grades in New Haven schools, *J. exp. Educ.*, 1938, *7*, 11–18.

Lambert, P., and others, A comparison of pupil achievement in team and self-contained organizations, *J. exp. Educ.*, 1965, *33*, 217–224.

Lathrop, I. I., Scholastic achievement at Iowa State College associated with high school size and course pattern, *J. exp. Educ.*, 1960, *29*, 37–48.

Leonard, J. P., and A. C. Eurich, *An evaluation of modern education*. New York: Appleton, 1942.

Leton, D. A., Analysis of high school general educational development test scores, *Calif. J. educ. Res.*, 1957, *8*, 214–218.

Lisonbee, L., and B. J. Fullerton, The comparative effect of BSCS and traditional biology on student achievement, *Sch. Sci. Math.*, 1964, *64*, 594–598.

Lumsdaine, A. A., Educational technology, programmed learning, and instructional science, *Yearb. Nat. Soc. Stud. Educ.*, 1964, *63*, Part I, 371–401.

McKeachie, W. J., Research on teaching at the college and university level, in N. L. Gage, ed., *Handbook of research on teaching*. Skokie, Ill.: Rand McNally, 1963, 1118–1172.

McKeachie, W. J., and others, Individualized teaching in elementary psychology, *J. educ. Psychol.*, 1960, *51*, 285–291.

McKenna, B. H., Greater learning in smaller classes, *NEA J.*, 1957, *46*, 437–438.

Marklund, S., Scholastic attainments as related to size and homogeneity of classes, *Educ. Res.*, 1963, *6*, 63–67.

Marr, J. N., and others, The contribution of the lecture to college teaching, *J. educ. Psychol.*, 1960, *51*, 277–284.

Medley, D. M., and H. E. Mitzel, Measuring classroom behavior by systematic observations, in N. L. Gage, ed., *Handbook of research on teaching*. Skokie, Ill.: Rand McNally, 1963, 247–328.

Milton, O., Two-year follow up: Objective data after learning without class attendance, *Psychol. Rep.*, 1962, *11*, 833–836.

Muir, N. D., A comparison of the competence in algebra of the grade IX students of the Edmonton public schools in 1938 and 1959, *Alberta J. educ. Res.*, 1961, *7*, 175–184.

Nachman, M., and S. Opochinsky, The effects of different teaching methods: a methodological study, *J. educ. Psychol.*, 1958, *49*, 245–249.

Newman, S. C., and R. L. Mooney, Effects of student self-help, *J. higher Educ.*, 1940, *11*, 435–442.

Noll, V. H., The effect of written tests upon achievement in college classes: An experiment and a summary of evidence, *J. educ. Res.*, 1939, *32*, 335–358.

Owen, S. G., and others, Programmed learning in medical education, *Postgraduate medical Journal*, 1965, *41*, 201.

Parsons, T. S., A comparison of instruction by kinescope, correspondence study, and customary classroom procedures, *J. educ. Psychol.*, 1957, *48*, 27–40.

Pattinson, W., Streaming in the schools, *Educ. Res.*, 1963, *5*, 229–235.

Peters, C. C., and W. R. Van Voorhis, *Statistical procedures and their mathematical bases*. New York: McGraw-Hill, 1940.

Popham, W. J., Tape recorded lectures in the college classroom II., *A-V Comm. Rev.*, 1962, *10*, 94–101.

Poppleton, Pamela K., and K. Austwick, A comparison of programmed learning and note-taking at two age levels, *Brit. J. educ. Psychol.*, 1964, *34*, 43–50.

Powell, J. P., Experimentation and teaching in higher education, *Educ. Res.*, 1964, *6*, 179–191.

Rainey, R. G., A comparison of the CHEM study curriculum and a conventional approach in teaching high school chemistry, *Sch. Sci. Math.*, 1964, *64*, 539–544.

Remmers, H. H., ed., Studies in extracurricular activities, *Purdue Univ. Stud. higher Educ.*, 1940, No. 39, pp. 16–30.

Ricciuti, E. A., Children and radio: a study of listeners and non-listeners to various types of radio programs in terms of selected ability, attitude and behavior measures, *Genet. Psychol. Monogr.*, 1951, *44*, 69–143.

Riley, J. W., B. E. Ryan, and Marcia Lipshitz. *The student looks at his teacher*. New Brunswick, N. J.: Rutgers University Press, 1950.

Ryans, D. G., The prediction of teacher effectiveness, *Encyclopedia of educational research*. New York: Macmillan, 1960, 1486–1491.

Ryans, D. G., Some observations concerning the relationship of time spent at study to scholarship and other factors, *J. educ. Psychol.*, 1939, *30*, 372–377.

Schoenhard, G. H., Home visitation put to a test, *Person. Guid. J.*, 1958, *36*, 480–485.

Schramm, W., Learning from instructional television, *Rev. educ. Res.*, 1962, *32*, 156–167.

Sears, Pauline S., and E. R. Hilgard, The teacher's role in the motivation of the learner, *Yearb. Nat. Soc. Stud. Educ.*, 1964, 63, Part I, 182–209.

Selakovitch, D., An experiment attempting to determine the effectiveness of frequent testing as an aid to learning in beginning college courses in American government, *J. educ. Res.*, 1962, *55*, 178–180.

Shaplin, J. T., and H. F. Olds, Jr., eds., *Team teaching*. New York: Harper & Row, 1964.

Shouksmith, G., and J. W. Taylor, The effects of counselling on the achievement of high-ability pupils, *Brit. J. educ. Psychol.*, 1964, *34*, 51–57.

Smith, H. L., and M. T. Eaton, Analysis of the proficiency in silent reading of 15,206 sixth-grade pupils in 648 schools in Indiana, *Bull. Sch. Educ. Indiana Univ.*, 1945, *21*, No. 6.

Standlee, L. W., and W. J. Popham, Quizzes' contribution to learning, *J. educ. Psychol.*, 1960, *51*, 322–325.

Stephens, J. M., and A. Lichtenstein, Factors associated with success in teaching grade-five arithmetic, *J. educ. Res.*, 1947, *40*, 683–694.

Stephens, J. M., *The influence of the school on the individual*. Ann Arbor, Mich.: Edwards Bros., 1933.

Stern, G. G., Measuring noncognitive variables in research on teaching, in N. L. Gage, ed., *Handbook of research on teaching*. Skokie, Ill.: Rand McNally, 1963, 398–447.

Stovall, T. F., Classroom methods: lecture vs discussion, *Phi Delta Kappan*, 1958, *39*, 255–258.

Strang, Ruth, *Behavior and background of students in college and secondary school*. New York: Harper & Row, 1937.

Street, P., J. H. Powell, and J. W. Hamblin, Achievement of students and size of school, *J. educ. Res.*, 1962, *55*, 261–266.

Svensson, N. E., Ability grouping and scholastic achievement: five-year follow-up study in Stockholm, *Educ. Res.*, 1962, *5*, 53–56.

Thompson, G. W., Children's acceptance of television advertising and the relation of televiewing to school achievement, *J. educ. Res.*, 1964, *58*, 171–174.

Tilton, J. W., An experimental effort to change the achievement test profile, *J. exp. Educ.*, 1947, *15*, 318–322.

Trueblood, D. L., Effects of employment on academic achievement, *Person. Guid. J.*, 1957, *36*, 112–115.

Wallen, N. E., and R. M. W. Travers, Analysis and investigation of teaching methods, in N. L. Gage, ed., *Handbook of research on teaching*. Skokie, Ill.: Rand McNally, 1963, 448–505.

White, R. W., How successful is team teaching?, *Sci. Teach.*, 1964 (Oct.), *31*, No. 6, 34–37.

Wilson, J. A. R., Differences in achievement attributable to different educational environments, *J. educ. Res.*, 1958, *52*, 83–93.

Winborn, B., and L. G. Schmidt, The effectiveness of short-term counseling upon the academic achievement of potentially superior but underachieving college freshmen, *J. educ. Res.*, 1962, *55*, 167–173.

Wiseman, S., *Education and environment*. Manchester, England: University of Manchester Press, 1964.

Wrightstone, J. W., *Evaluating achievement in basic skills in newer vs conventional schools: A summary of major research studies*. A report to the Childhood Education Committee of the Governor's Fact-Finding Commission on Education, 1951. Mimeographed, 13 pp.

Zweibelson, I., M. Bahnmuller, and L. Lyman, Team teaching and flexible grouping in the junior high school social studies, *J. exp. Educ.*, 1965, *34*, 20–32.

PART THREE

IMPLICATIONS AND ELABORATIONS

8 | THE EFFECTIVE TEACHER:

His Characteristics and His Place in Society

In the materials developed so far, much has been implied about the effective teacher. We have examined the spontaneous tendencies held to be sufficient for much of teaching (Chapter 6). We have seen the nature of the task for which the teacher is responsible (Chapter 3), and we have noticed some general data (Chapter 7) suggesting that many of the traditional parameters of teaching seem to have little relation to effectiveness in the art.

In this section we consider the implications in more detail and apply them to the teacher as a person. We ask: What kind of person is likely to carry out these tasks and to give expression to these spontaneous tendencies? Can we see, within one person, the concerns and the propensities that would make for effective teaching?

With few exceptions, the discussion consists almost exclusively of deductions from the theory. In spite of the vast amount of research on teacher effectiveness, few of the data are relevant, and of those still fewer are consistent (Rosencranz and Biddle, 1964). There is a widely held belief that useful data will have to wait for the appearance of systematic theory. There is a hope, therefore, that deductions from a theory such as ours may facilitate the actual gathering of useful data.

Knowledge of a Special Subject Matter

To induce learning in his charges, the teacher must bring to their attention the subject matter to be learned. He must also lead the pupils to make some response to various aspects of the subject. He must reinforce some of these responses and refrain from reinforcing others. He must, on occasion, guide the pupil into an adequate response that presently escapes the pupil. He should be so constituted that he will sharpen the pupil's insight into the fact that a certain way of behaving leads to a given result.

The teacher could do these things either from a deliberate resolve, or from automatic, spontaneous urges, or from any combinations of these. The theory of schooling holds that effective teaching will be more dependable insofar as the necessary actions come from natural, spontaneous forces.

The subject matter professed by the teacher, it will be remembered (Chapter 4), is chiefly the subject matter which other people regard with moderate, perhaps indulgent, approval but for which they feel only occasional and passing concern. To bring these academic subjects before his students in sustained fashion, the teacher himself must have some knowledge of the subject and the willingness, preferably the urge, to entertain the basic ideas in the subject. It is true, of course, that teachers who are lacking in knowledge of their subject can still arrange for necessary stimulation by using other resources or by various indirect means. This ability to invoke sources beyond the teacher's own knowledge can at times be most important, especially in advanced work, or in stimulating children at any level to engage in special interests. For most teaching, however, these outside sources are not considered a dependable substitute for the teacher's knowledge of subject matter.

Little will be said here about just how much the teacher should know about his subject. For day-in and day-out teaching, it would seem helpful if he knew as much as his best pupil is likely to learn, and prudence calls for a comfortable margin beyond this. But as far as stimulation is concerned, we cannot hold that the more knowledge the better, and certainly we cannot expect a linear relation between knowledge of subject and skill in teaching.

The actual data in this area are most confusing, and it is difficult to point out any systematic trends (Barr and others, 1961; Domas and Tiedeman, 1950; Morsh and Wilder, 1954; Ryans, 1960. See Biddle and Ellena, 1964 for additional references). More often than not there is a slight positive relation between knowledge of subject and success in teaching. But the relation is by no means consistent and is seldom large. There is a possibility that the relation is more marked at the secondary level than at the elementary school level. Worcester (1961), in his review of the famous Wisconsin studies, suggests that, at the high school level, the effectiveness of the teacher is more accurately predicted by his *high school* standing in the subject being taught than by his later college standing in the same subject. Perhaps it is chiefly important that the teacher be meticulously versed in the material with which the student is expected to grapple.

Along with his knowledge and a personal interest in his subject, the teacher must have the willingness, preferably the compulsion, to talk to others about his subject. It is not at all necessary that the communication be undertaken for altruistic purposes. Indeed we would expect more dependable teaching from the person who, in talking about his subject, was driven by the same compulsion the traveler feels when he tells of his journeys or by an urge similar to that of the parent who talks to all and sundry about the doings of his child. It is somewhat ironic that the terms we use to describe the successful teacher come perilously close to describing the bore.

Students often use trial-and-error procedures. That is, they react to an idea, a situation, or a problem several times before they reach an acceptable response. If the trial-and-error procedure is to be effective, the teacher must be willing to keep an idea, situation, or problem before the students long enough to permit a series of responses. He should not merely mention one idea and rush on to another one while the students are frantically reacting to the first. He must linger, preferably in a dignified manner. A lecturer, for instance, may hold an idea before an audience by repeating it in slightly different form, stating it one way and then another way, each statement being designed to elicit a new reaction.

The willingness to dwell on simple ideas may spring largely from ordinary patience. But it is not entirely a matter of patience. As conceived here, the willingness to linger over elementary ideas does not necessarily imply kindness, or gentleness, or consideration for the learner. It may come from sheer repetitiveness, or slowness, or love of one's own words. The willingness to linger is the important thing. The underlying motive is not specified.

Willingness to linger over ideas does not always go hand in hand with exceptional scholarship. The accomplished scholar may be reluctant to keep an idea, particularly an elementary idea, before his students. The elementary idea has no appeal to him as an idea. He is on the trail of a much more intriguing, more subtle, more complex idea just around the corner. It may be exceedingly hard for him to dwell on a seemingly elementary concept when he has something really important to say. This is one consideration that makes us unwilling to predict teaching.

a one-to-one relationship between knowledge of subject and skill in

Reinforcement

The teacher must motivate, stimulate, or set ideas in motion. He must also reinforce. As we have noted, he must accept some reactions that his pupils make to the ideas he sets forth. Other reactions he must not accept. What qualities must the teacher have to master this differential reinforcement?

To a certain extent, the qualities needed for applying reinforcement duplicate those needed for effective stimulation. If the teacher is to know which ideas to accept and which to reject, he must know his subject. Indeed, the mastery required for reinforcement is probably much greater than the mastery required for the original presentation. Preparation for the presentation can be made in advance with the help of textbook and references. No facile and wide-ranging mastery is necessary. Reinforcement, however, cannot be anticipated. The teacher must react to the student's responses as he makes them, guided by information on tap at the moment.

Preferably the teacher's knowledge of subject matter should be so ingrained that it controls the many automatic reinforcements that continually come from the subtle changes of expression on the teacher's face. As the pupil's statements hit home, the teacher's face shows pleasure or relief; as the pupil strays into more questionable territory, the teacher looks puzzled, uncomprehending, or hurt. These subtle changes spring automatically to the teacher's countenance. They are seldom deliberate. But they will come only if the teacher has a fairly rich background of information so clearly in mind that the pupil's statements elicit inevitable reactions.

These automatic expressions provide some measure of reinforcement whether the teacher intends them to or not. But they are not enough. The teacher must be willing, preferably compelled, to apply overt reinforcement as well.

This willingness to apply reinforcement comes most readily from the person who is uncomfortable in the presence of error. When he hears a mistake, he is impelled to correct. He corrects the grammatical slip. He contests the seeming error of fact. He comments on the clumsy management of an instrument. The compulsion to correct may function even in the face of a resolve to remain silent. Reinforcement that springs from such compulsion is likely to be inevitable and prompt. In contrast, the reinforcement that arises chiefly from a deliberate resolve or a sense of obligation may suffer the fate of other good intentions—postponement or neglect.

Guidance and the Sharpening of Insight

It is not enough for the teacher to stimulate pupils and to reinforce their behavior. He must also guide his charges into the correct way of behaving. To perform this function, it is chiefly necessary that the teacher share the widespread urge to supply the answer for which someone else is groping. Like the onlookers in a quiz contest, he must feel a compulsion to blurt out the answer that eludes the participant. He must be inclined to rush in and supply the answer to his own rhetorical questions. True enough, there are times when the sophisticated teacher will strive firmly to suppress this powerful urge. His rational processes will call upon him to inhibit his tendency to supply the answer and will ask that he stand patiently aside while the pupil works things out for himself. But such a deliberate resolve suggests that there is a powerful urge to be controlled. And even though some restraint may occasionally be in order, this spontaneous impulse to supply the answer, will serve, in the long run, as the basis for much effective teaching.

Our theory demands that, at times, the teacher shall be led to sharpen the pupil's insight, to show that this result follows from that way of behaving. To meet this demand, it is again merely necessary that the teacher be well supplied with the tendencies to point the moral, to say, "see what happens when you do things this way!"

A sense of mission, it will be remembered, is not demanded by the theory. The intensity of this sense of mission would undoubtedly affect the operation of the spontaneous factors. For a complete theory of the teacher, this dimension must be investigated. In working out the deductions from the spontaneous factors, however, this dimension of deliberate mission does not play a vital part.

The General Relations between Teacher and Pupil

In much of what has been said, there is a clear implication that the teacher will count in some way with the pupils. To stimulate or motivate the pupils, he must be listened to or attended to. If his approval or disapproval is to have any effect, he must be the kind of person whose approval or disapproval matters to children. If he is to sharpen the insight of pupils, he must be the kind of person whose comments are taken seriously.

For the purposes of the theory, it is the pupils who must take the teacher seriously. True enough, we would expect that the traits which made the teacher count with pupils would also account for a certain amount of acceptance among adults. There are times, however, when this does not follow. It is possible for a teacher to be quite a personage to his pupils and yet be written off as a nonentity by parents or other adults. Conversely, a person who impresses adults may have little impact on the pupils. In the case of such disparity, it is the impact on the pupils that should be stressed.

There are many ways in which a teacher can be taken seriously. He can be loved. He can be admired. He can be feared. He can be seen as a symbol of some agency that is taken seriously. But by one means or another he must count. He cannot be disregarded.

What does the theory have to say about the teacher's liking for children? Obviously the theory demands that the teacher must be willing, preferably impelled, to consort with children, to communicate with them, and to attend to their activities. The simplest way to make sure of these tendencies is to provide the teacher with a genuine liking for children and an equally genuine concern for their welfare.

But this liking for children is not a strict or necessary deduction from the theory. Although fondness for children would perhaps be the most economical device, and certainly the most pleasant device, to ensure adequate contact between teacher and student, it is by no means the only device. Effective contact could be made and effective teaching accomplished by the outright egotist who simply regarded children as a convenient audience, or as a collective instrument that echoed back to him his own beloved sentiments, or as mere vessels to catch in decent fashion the overflow of his own great learning. Undoubtedly, vigorous and effective teaching has also been accomplished by those who regarded their pupils merely as so many potential tallies on the credit side of some celestial register.

Just as the theory fails to demand that the teacher should be fond of children, so it also fails to specify that he have any great understanding of children in general or of his own pupils in particular. Most of the spontaneous mechanisms could be used quite effectively by a person who was completely ignorant of the needs, concerns, problems, or aspirations of his pupils. Such an insensitive teacher does little to elicit our admiration or enthusiasms. But however much a degree of understanding may be demanded by considerations of humanity or decency, it is not a requirement that follows in strict logic from the theory itself.

Although the teacher's understanding of children is not a direct demand of the theory, it is possible that some knowledge of child nature may help the teacher in his general impact on pupils. In being completely oblivious to the workings of children's minds, the teacher might so reduce his social force that pupils would fail to be influenced by his statements or by his approval or disapproval. In this indirect fashion, accordingly, the teacher's understanding of child nature may play a part in effectiveness.

As in so many other matters, the empirical evidence on this question is somewhat ambiguous. Clearly, however, the evidence does not suggest that a more intimate knowledge of one's own pupils will regularly lead to more effective teaching. One early study (Ojemann and Wilkinson, 1939) did report some gains from having teachers learn more about their pupils. A later, more sophisticated study (Hoyt, 1955), however, found no gains in achievement from such an increased understanding on the part of the teacher. Hoyt did find, however, that with such increased understanding some pupils acquired a more favorable attitude toward the teacher. In his general review of the literature, Bush (1958) held that the advantage coming from the teacher's understanding of his pupils, even when present, is by no means pronounced.

The Teacher in the Eyes of Adults

At several places in this discussion, the qualities attributed to the successful teacher have carried some unflattering overtones. We have held that the successful teacher is keenly and consistently interested in many subjects for which other people feel only passing concern. With little or no provocation, the natural teacher holds forth on esoteric or academic topics, lingering lovingly over elementary details. He is impelled, to an unusual extent, to comment on what others may say about the subject of his interest. He finds it difficult to keep from correcting the mistakes of others, even when no practical purpose is served by the correction.

The actual demands of the theory would be met if the teacher exhibited these traits only in the presence of juniors or potential students, laying them aside when he met with fellow adults for ordinary social purposes. But the ability to turn the tendencies on and off is not specified. On the contrary, the tendencies are more likely to function if they are spontaneous and compulsive. This feature makes it extremely likely that many good teachers will exhibit the necessary traits even after school hours.

There is always the hope that the more dreary tendencies may be made more palatable by such qualities as enthusiasm and the ability to see unusual relations in everyday aspects of the subject. But this is not likely to provide a major remedy.

In stressing the risks to which teachers are exposed through the very traits essential to our craft, the theory is in line with a substantial segment of folklore (Belok and Dowling, 1961; Charles, 1950; Furness, 1962) and with some empirical evidence. "Teacher" is the epithet that Eliza Doolittle hurls at Professor Higgins when his repeated corrections drive her beyond endurance. "Miss Schoolteacher" is the rebuke administered to Bella Goss when her overly corrected mother feels she must retaliate. Sober studies, moreover, report a feeling of social ostracism or lack of acceptance on the part of many teachers. In several reports (Charters, 1963; Havighurst and Neugarten, 1962), teachers are not considered as part of the normal adult world but are treated somewhat as a race apart. In introducing an ordinary adult, for instance, one speaks of "My friend, Mrs. Jones." If the adult is a teacher, however, she is likely to be introduced as, "Harry's teacher, Mrs. Jones."

In the popular mind, the rather unflattering stereotype of the teacher still persists (Rosencranz and Biddle, 1964). Middle-class mothers, in guessing at the need-system of teachers, suggest the domineering, self-centered pedagogue, obsessed with the need of keeping minor details in conventional order (Saltz, 1960).

The traditional teacher stereotype may be changing somewhat. O'Dowd and Beardslee (1961) report that college students stress the teacher's dedication to culture and the arts and his self-sacrifice. But they still present the male teacher as mild, unassertive, underpaid, and uninfluential in the community. Current literary descriptions of individual teachers do not follow the earlier stereotype in any detail. Many recent writers, however, feel safe in using the earlier stereotype as an effective image (Wolf, 1961). Like the fictional characters of Falstaff or Don Quixote, the term "typical teacher" will conjure up a vivid picture. Even though the more recent author may modify the image in his own treatment, he finds that he can use the stereotype as an economical reference point.

Closely linked with the unflattering stereotype of the teacher as a person, there is the problem of the lowly prestige of teaching. This phenomenon of lowly prestige, so often decried, and so regularly reported (Charters, 1963), is also rendered less mysterious, although perhaps no less disturbing, by some of the ideas developed in the theory of spontaneous schooling. The ideas in question are to be found both in the general speculations about the origins of schools and in the more rigorous treatment of the forces at work within the schools.

Consider the contrast between the work of the teacher and that of the figure whose prestige the teacher so often envies—the physician. The physician works primarily with those aspects of life that have urgent survival value (Chapter 3) and that are seldom deferrable. He intercedes between us and some serious menace. Typically he acts in the face of present distress or urgent immediate danger.

The teacher, in contrast, works largely with those traits for which the home feels a remote, and indulgent concern. Even when parents do get around to feeling some worry about the child's academic well-being, they feel no panic-stricken urge to telephone the teacher at 11:30 P.M. and beg for remedial treatment. The treatment, however badly it is needed, can wait until tomorrow or even until the day after tomorrow.

This more indulgent and lackadaisical attitude to matters in the teacher's domain may be furthered by the fact that academic ills are seldom as obvious and dramatic as many physical ailments. It is difficult to ignore the difference between sickness and health or between the broken leg and its normal counterpart. Academic deficiencies, on the other hand, seldom call attention to themselves in this dramatic fashion. Far from being obvious, they must be sought out by elaborate test and probe. And the person who deals with these hidden blemishes may readily occupy a less conspicuous place in the minds of the general public.

To some extent, then, the basic sociological function of the teacher would invite or permit an element of neglect or nonchalance in the public attitude toward teaching and teachers. Along with the neglect stemming from the sociological function of the school, moreover, there may be additional disregard to be expected from the classroom mechanisms employed by the teacher. These basic mechanisms, according to the spontaneous theory, are not those of the surgeon, nor those involved in the intricate manipulation of atomic materials. These basic mechanisms in teaching, on the contrary, are more similar to those of the gardener or of the ordinary mother. To a certain extent, the teacher remains in general contact with maturing organisms and exerts general pressure in one direction rather than another. However much his techniques may ultimately be enhanced by finesse and delicate adjustments, they are basically rather general in nature.

It would be amazing, of course, if the general public has a clearly structured view of the doctrines set forth in the theory of spontaneous schooling. But however slightly the layman may understand the theory, he may have learned from generations of neglect that he can afford to take an indulgent attitude toward teaching without risking disaster. In this, as in most matters, people can act effectively on principles that they only dimly comprehend.

Does all this imply a callous gloating over the unfortunate plight in which many teachers may find themselves? Surely not! To describe an evil or a discomfort and to try to understand it, is not to condone or to welcome it. If teachers experience some measure of rejection, a searching and honest inquiry into possible causes would seem the most valuable first step. All in all, it seems much more helpful to see this misfortune, if it exists, as the logical result of powerful and widespread forces, than to spend our time in protesting, complaining, and condemning. When some understanding is attained, we should be in a much better position to see what might be done. The present analysis does suggest a certain inevitability, but this is only a general analysis. A complete analysis might reveal many ways in which the basic mechanisms might be used for their valuable outcomes, but modified to reduce undesirable side effects.

All in all, these spontaneous tendencies are by no means least among the forces that enable the teacher to carry out his task. Earthy and ordinary as they are, they might well be acknowledged and, when necessary, used as the basis for further refinements.

REFERENCES

Barr, A. S., and others, Wisconsin studies of the measurement and prediction of teacher effectiveness: a summary of investigations, *J. exp. Educ.*, 1961, *30*, 5–156.

Belok, M., and F. R. Dowling, Teacher image and the teacher shortage, *Phi Delta Kappan*, 1961, *42*, 255–256.

Biddle, B. J., and W. J. Ellena, eds., *Contemporary research on teacher effectiveness*. New York: Holt, Rinehart and Winston, Inc., 1964.

Bush, R. N., The human relations factor: I. principles of successful teacher-pupil relationship, *Phi Delta Kappan*, 1958, *39*, 271–273.

Charles, D. C., The stereotype of the teacher in American literature, *Ed. Forum*, 1950, *14*, 299–305.

Charters, W. W., Jr., The social background of teaching, in N. L. Gage, ed., *Handbook of research on teaching*. Skokie, Ill.: Rand McNally, 1963, 715–813.

Domas, S. J., and D. Tiedeman, Teacher competence: an annotated bibliography, *J. exp. Educ.*, 1950, *19*, 101–218.

Furness, Edna L., Portrait of the pedagogue in eighteenth century England, *Hist. Educ. Quart.*, 1962, *2*, 62–70.

Havighurst, R. J., and Bernice L. Neugarten, *Society and education*, second ed. Boston: Allyn and Bacon, 1962.

Hoyt, K. B., A study of the effects of teacher knowledge of pupil characteristics on pupil achievement and attitudes towards classwork, *J. educ. Psychol.*, 1955, *46*, 302–310.

Morsh, J. E., and E. W. Wilder, Identifying the effective instructor: a review of quantitative studies, 1900–1952. Research Bulletin No. AFPTRC-TR-54–44. San Antonio, Tex.: USAF Personnel and Training Center, 1954.

O'Dowd, D. D., and D. C. Beardslee, The student image of the school teacher, *Phi Delta Kappan*, 1961, *42*, 250–254.

Ojemann, R. H., and F. R. Wilkinson, The effect on pupil growth of an increase in teacher's understanding of pupil behavior, *J. exp. Educ.*, 1939, *8*, 143–147.

Rosencranz, H. A., and B. J. Biddle, The role approach to teacher competence, in B. J. Biddle and W. J. Ellena, eds., *Contemporary research on teacher effectiveness.* New York: Holt, Rinehart and Winston, Inc., 1964.

Ryans, D. G., Prediction of teacher effectiveness, *Encyclopedia of educational research,* third ed. New York: Macmillan, 1960.

Saltz, Joanne W., Teacher stereotype: liability in recruiting?, *Sch. Rev.,* 1960, *68,* 105–111.

Smith, C. E., Educational research and the preparation of teachers. Vancouver, Canada: British Columbia Teachers' Federation, 1962–1963.

Wolf, T. L., The teacher in the contemporary American novel, Master's essay (Education), The Johns Hopkins University, 1961.

Worcester, D. A., Some assumptions, explicitly and implicitly made, in the investigations here summarized, *J. exp. Educ.,* 1961, *30,* 120–133.

9 | THE SCHOOL'S SUCCESS IN DIFFERENT TASKS

At several points in the development of this theory, it has been held that the basic tools of the school are geared to the traditional function speculatively attributed to the school. Can the school, then, lightly change its role? If it does take on new tasks or new functions, how much success can it expect in converting its old tools for the new tasks? Are the basic mechanisms available to the school so versatile that they can be used for any task to which the school may turn its hand? Or are they highly specialized mechanisms, well suited to perform some functions but clumsy and awkward when used for other tasks?

In the past, unfortunately, many people inside the schools and out have ignored these questions and have blithely assumed that the school could take over almost any task, if only it would. Indeed, we have suspected inertia or laziness behind the school's preoccupation with academic matters, and behind its stubborn and regrettable refusal to take on the responsibility for developing character and an integrated way of life.

To approach this problem in a clear-cut fashion, we must again lean on the speculations regarding the origins of the school. Let us suppose that the school has undertaken a series of tasks that vary in the immediacy of their survival value (Chapter 3). One of these tasks, such as that of teaching a pupil how to square a binomial, has rather remote survival value. A second, such as inducing respect for property, has somewhat more immediate survival value, whereas a third, the reasonable management of sexual relations, deals with an area even farther to the immediacy end of our gradient.

What factors should we take into account in estimating the probability of the school's success in these tasks?

The Role of Maturation

Although not a tool of the school, maturation is one of the most important factors to be taken into account when estimating the probable success of the school. For success in any task, the school must assume a certain degree of maturation in its pupils. Teaching the square of a binomial, for instance, would present stupendous difficulties if attempted in grade two or three. It would present much less difficulty to a student in grade eleven or twelve, even if the student had never before studied mathematics. The same is true for the nonacademic subjects. It would be difficult to teach a four-year-old how to drive a car properly or how to react to a member of the opposite sex in adult yet seemly fashion.

For some traits maturation, having made learning possible, may go no further. It may give the child the power to behave in one way or in the other way, but it may influence him no more toward one of those ways than toward the other. A certain amount of maturation is necessary before the child can learn to eat, but maturation may have nothing to do with the child's choice of eating either snails or cottage cheese. A further degree of maturation may enable him to talk, but whether he talks in the manner of Boston or in the fashion of Atlanta is not a matter for maturation. In this latter respect, maturation is strictly neutral.

But maturation is not always strictly neutral. For some traits maturation not only makes it possible for the child to do the right thing or the wrong thing, but it may strongly incline him to do the one rather than the other. Maturation not only makes it possible for the boy either to drive slowly or to speed. It may also incline him toward speeding. Maturation not only makes it possible for the boy either to entertain his "date" in decorous fashion or to indulge in undesirable intimacies. It may make the latter behavior more attractive. Maturation not only makes it possible for the child either to play with the gang, on the one hand, or to sit absorbed with his own thoughts, but it may also make him favor the more gregarious behavior.

The net influence of the school should be greatest when maturation is strictly neutral. The development of the child will be most responsive to the school's influence when maturation merely makes it possible for him to behave either one way or the other but does not push him toward one way rather than another. The school should be most effective when maturation merely "develops" him to a point at which he can be led to perform either the desired or the undesired behavior. If maturation pushes the child toward the undesired behavior (uninhibited sexual behavior), the school will find itself in actual conflict with a powerful force. If, on the other hand, maturation pushes the child toward the acceptable behavior (the eight-year-old playing with his fellows), the school becomes partially superfluous, and its active efforts will show little in the way of observable net returns. If, on the contrary, maturation makes either behavior possible ($a^2 + 2ab + b^2$ instead of $a^2 + b^2$) and then retires to a neutral corner, the school is left a free field in pushing the child toward the preferred answer.

According to the sociological speculations in the theory of spontaneous schooling, (Chapter 3), it is inevitable, of course, that maturation shall take a more partisan attitude in the development of behavior that has more immediate survival value. During the time that our species was evolving it was not enough for maturation to permit the male either to approach the female or, on the other hand, to avoid her. He must be strongly impelled to approach. It would not be enough that maturation would permit the young child either to remain in solitude or to play with his fellows. He should be impelled toward gregarious activities.

In contrast to this fierce, no-nonsense, partisan role of maturation in the middle portion of the gradient, there is no corresponding necessity that maturation take a partisan attitude toward the diatonic musical scale or toward the merits of cursive script. In these areas, having exceedingly remote survival value, it is quite in order that maturation should make possible any one of many different ways of behaving but should remain indifferent as to which way is chosen.

There is a second, somewhat controversial, aspect of maturation that may introduce problems for character education. According to the theories of Freud and of Piaget, character development proceeds through a series of identifiable stages. Certain types of character controls can be acquired during one stage but would be exceedingly difficult, if not impossible, to teach at an early stage. Conversely, a control that is not acquired during the appropriate stage may be difficult to develop thereafter.

If the Freudians in particular should be right, moreover, much of the general shaping of character has taken place long before the child first comes to school. Many of the details, of course, are still to be worked out during the school years, but the structure of the superego has already been determined, the child has already worked out his patterns of identification and has established a basic style for dealing with his urges with his relations to others and with his relations with himself.

Although this aspect of maturation should be mentioned, it will not receive major stress. The whole concept of stages is still enmeshed in controversy, and the Freudian theories especially are seriously questioned (Jones, 1960; Murphy, 1962). It is an open question, moreover, whether the concept of stages poses more problems for character education than for academic proficiency.

The Specialized Interests of the Teacher

In our speculations regarding the probable origins of the school, we have made much of the fact that teachers are a specialized group with respect to academic matters. More than the average citizen, the teacher has a continuing interest in many matters with remote survival value. Day in and day out, teachers are unusually concerned with the expansion of a binomial, with the intricacies of the gerundive construction, and with the constitution of the Greek city-state. It seems safe to assume that, because of the ancient distribution of responsibility, any process of selecting teachers is bound to secure people with better than average competence in the academic subjects. The typical teacher of algebra may not know enough about his subject to make the expert happy. However, he is far ahead of the general population in this respect.

With respect to character, on the other hand, there is no automatic procedure to guarantee unusual competence in teachers. True enough, we take steps to exclude the markedly unfit. But our procedures are not designed to make sure that teachers exceed the general public in courage, kindliness, or magnaminity.

Engaging the Mechanisms of Learning

It has been held (Chapter 6) that the spontaneous tendencies in the teacher are bound to engage the basic mechanisms of learning to be found in the child and thus are bound to induce a measure of attainment in academic areas. Does this necessity hold equally in the more vital areas of character or social decency?

If the child is to master algebra, something must be done to bring algebraic matters to his attention and to be sure he will be moderately alert when these things are part of his experience. This is the problem of *motivation*. Successful motivation in algebra hinges largely on the expression of the teacher's or the school's concern for this subject. With no expression or with inadequate expression of the teacher's specialized concern, we might expect little development in this area. With effective expression, we would have at least taken the first step toward such development.

Unless the teacher does something about it, the child may never be stimulated or motivated to deal with the square of a binomial or with the intricacies of the Latin gerundive. But we will surely not find this to be the case when we turn to the more vital areas of character or social relations. With or without the teacher's interest, the child is bound to encounter many situations that are important in the realm of character of social adjustment. Whether the teacher does anything about it or not, the child will be deluged with temptations to cheat or steal, with opportunities to fight or retreat, or to seek some other alternative, and with choices between facing a menace or resorting to fantasy. In this area, unlike the academic area, there would be much stimulation without the intervention of the teacher.

The individual problems that constitute the character curriculum will assail the child whether or not the teacher takes a hand. *Practice* in these problems, moreover, will occur at times of their own choosing and, at times, may fail to fit into the sequence determined by the teacher. Insofar as a graded series of tasks is important to learning, we can expect the teaching of character to be under a serious handicap.

The mechanism of *reinforcement* can also be expected to work differently in teaching such a thing as sexual prudence than in teaching algebraic processes. There are many *intriguing subsequent events* that distinguish sexual acts from sexual restraint. Many of these intriguing, subsequent events have strong physiological components, and these completely elude the teacher's control. The consequences which differentiate an algebraic error from an acceptable response, on the other hand, are almost entirely social and symbolic and are almost completely under the teacher's control. Most of the algebraic behavior will be under the teacher's eye, and he can apply as rigid a schedule of reinforcement as he chooses. This is not true for sexual behavior. In applying his schedule of reinforcement to algebraic responses, the teacher encounters little competition from other people or other agencies. If other agencies do contest his decision about the adequacy of a response, the teacher has abundant prestige to bolster his position in these matters. In sexual behavior the teacher has no such monopoly of social reinforcement. Other people may readily comment on what the pupil does or fails to do in sexual matters. If such comments conflict with those of the teacher, the latter can seldom pass as an unquestioned authority in the world of sex or romance.

Reinforcement should be more effective if it is forceful and unequivocal. It is likely to lose some of its impact if it is administered in an uncertain, hemming-and-hawing manner. And, as it happens, there can often be less flat-footed conviction in the realm of character education than in the area of academic attainment.

Compared to academic goals, the goals of character education are extremely difficult to determine. When a pupil faces a situation such as "$7 + 6 = ?$," or "Influence of the frontier," or "Results of the Industrial Revolution," or "Arma virumque cano," we have a fairly definite idea of the proper or acceptable response. Within limits, most teachers would agree as to the type of reaction they would try to induce. When a child faces social or ethical problems, on the other hand, we may be less certain about the desirable response. What should a child do, for instance, if he is playing with an attractive toy and another child tries to take it away from him? What should he do if he is in the middle of an engrossing novel and is asked by a friend to come over and help with some project? What should a student do who is confronted with the desire to be elected to a fraternity? Should he deliberately cultivate the important people, polishing apples whenever possible and expressing interest which he does not feel? Or should he continue to be natural and sincere and let the chips fall where they may?

The uncertainties of character education are not confined to these immediate transient problems. The whole problem of the desirable personality or temperament has vexed mankind ever since the race has been articulate, and the answers have varied from century to century, from culture to culture, and from wise man to wise man. The vigorous, aggressive, bumptious extrovert who receives the adulation of one culture may be regarded with horror by a different group. The shy, restrained individual who expresses himself in subtle understatements may receive the sincere appreciation of one society and yet may be regarded as an insignificant nincompoop if he moves to other shores. It is hard to imagine a schoolman having the audacity or effrontery to settle these questions for a given child. The decisions are simply too important, too frightening. Shall we, for instance, transform our pupil into a gullible enthusiast who will rush off to the nearest barricade in the support of causes trumped up by cynical political manipulators? Or shall we have him turn out to be a blasé sophisticate to whom any call of the oppressed or any threat of evil is just more propaganda? Who of us, even if he had the power, would take it on himself to eliminate from future generations the Micawbers, the Falstaffs, the Tam O'Shanters, or the host of less renowned but amiable rogues who have added color to our lives? Who of us, on the other hand, would deliberately earmark certain of our charges for these unenviable but diverting roles?

Truly the development of character, or personality, or of social behavior is complicated for the teacher. Here he can feel none of the assurance that he experiences when he holds forth on the exports of Malay or on the square of the hypotenuse.

The Trend of the Evidence

When he looks at the evidence, the teacher of reading or arithmetic can find much reason for optimism. Some success is the rule. True enough, many onlookers will claim that the gains are disappointing in their extent. But no one can truthfully claim that there is no gain whatever. In the area of character, on the other hand, the picture is quite different. It is true, of course, that we do not find unrelieved failure. But in contrast to the reports for the academic subjects, we do find that accomplishment is exceedingly precarious (V. Jones, 1954, 1960). We encounter some successes, but there are many reports of no gain whatever. And the gains that do appear are often exceedingly modest in contrast to the changes that can be attributed to other agencies. Peck and Havighurst (1960), for instance, estimate that the school can hardly hope for one tenth of the influence exerted by the home. And certainly there is much more resemblance between the attitudes of pupils and their parents than between the attitudes of pupils and their teachers. Representative partial correlations between the attitudes of pupils and parents range from .60 to .75, whereas similar partial correlations between the attitudes of pupils and teachers range from .12 to .24 (Weltman and Remmers, 1946).

We must not intimate that attitude and character are immune to influence from outside the home. Ever since the classical investigations of Peterson and Thurstone (1933), it has been clear that highly charged motion pictures can bring about changes in attitude toward other nationalities. In these investigations, the motion pictures were powerful dramas, telling a convincing story for its own sake. There was no conspicuous preaching or pointing of the moral. Films overtly discussing the importance of better Negro-white relations (Kraus, 1962) have also proved effective. Studies of persuasion (Hovland, 1963), moreover, have shown that a single forceful lecture at times can alter the views of students toward specific political or international issues.

Our cautions regarding the limited success of the school in character training are directed not so much to the single dramatic episode that may occur in a school setting as to the sustained incorporation of such a topic within the regular curriculum of the school. In his summary of the early literature, Lichtenstein (1934) surveyed some thirty-one studies of this type. He found almost a perfect balance between those which reported some success in character education and those which reported failures. Lichtenstein, in his own investigation, found that the stressing of the scientific attitude in grade-six classes did reduce superstitions. Corresponding stress, however, did not reduce general prejudice or bring about an increase in scientific attitude in this grade. In the famous Jacob summary (1957) of some 350 separate studies, we find little change in attitude during the entire college period. And any change that did occur could seldom be attributed to specific courses designed to induce such a change. The Jacob report, although supported by many later writers (Freedman, 1960; McClintock and Turner, 1962) has not gone completely unchallenged (Webster and others, 1962). Specific college courses have been reported to induce different attitudes with respect to the precise subject matter of the courses (for example, highway safety; attitude to mental patients; attitude to child-rearing practices) (Coslin and Kerr, 1962; Merril, 1962). With regard to broad general attitudes, however, the results are mixed, to say the least.

Reports of the influence of the schools on combating prejudice also present mixed results. With increased schooling, we find a decrease in those prejudices that are an affront to the general intellect (e.g. the belief that there are differences between white and Negro blood; that Jews are tricky), but we cannot be sure that education will bring a more general tolerant attitude or a warmer personal acceptance of minority groups (Stember, 1961). In some southern regions, college seniors are more anti-Negro than are the freshmen (Young and others, 1960). In northern California, however, there are reports of reduction of anti-minority feeling with college experience (Plant, 1959).

There are few data on the effect of the school's attack on delinquency. We know, of course, that in communities with good schools there is less delinquency (Dell, 1963). But this may come from other factors, such as a decent standard of living, that are characteristic of good communities. Careful community attacks on delinquency, administered either through the schools (Tait and Hodges, 1962) or through counselors apart from the schools (McCord and McCord, 1959), have produced most discouraging results. In the Tait and Hodges study, there is a suggestion, fortunately not statistically significant, that the treated group had a higher record of delinquency.

The Cultivation of the More Vital Areas

Turning now from the grim data to the more general speculations regarding the evolution of the school, we note the claim that the academic areas traditionally nurtured by the school have only a remote claim as promoters of survival. This remoteness of survival values is the characteristic which distinguishes the academic concerns on the one hand from the areas of real life on the other. If this distinction is taken seriously, it follows automatically that, on the occasion of grim choice, the academic should yield to the vital. We hope, of course, that there will be no necessity for such a grim choice. We hope that we will not have to decide, for instance, between geometry and honesty. But if we do, honesty must be given a higher priority. Without some modicum of this commodity we would be headed for immediate disaster. Without geometry we would have a longer period of grace.

But to say that real life traits are more immediately important than academic traits is not to say that the school should take on the responsibility for teaching these more important things. On the contrary, indeed, we might wonder if these vital areas should be handed over to an institution that had evolved specifically as the custodian of the areas with less immediate importance.

During the long period in which schools were evolving, the typical parent could readily trust the school to determine what his son thinks of Alcibiades or of the anatomy of the crayfish. In the first place, our parent could feel that, even if the things taught were occasionally the wrong things, no tremendous harm would be done. People have managed to go through life with mistaken ideas about Alcibiades or in complete ignorance of that worthy personage. In these areas of remote survival value, fortunately, society can tolerate a certain amount of error. In the second place, our parent could feel reassured that most of the things taught in the academic areas would actually be the right things. Teachers, after all, are a selected group with respect to these matters, and, as we have stressed so often, the teacher has ordinarily surpassed the average citizen in his mastery of academic subjects.

In asking the school to be responsible for the character of his child, however, the typical parent could have no such reassurance. In the first place, according to our theory, he cannot be so indulgent with respect to an occasional failure in this more vital area. Serious defect here would be disastrous. In the second place, as pointed out earlier, he could not legitimately assume that teachers have been a selected group with respect to many positive aspects of character.

In suggesting that teachers as a group may have only average status in character and in the more vital aspects of behavior, we are clearly in the realm of speculation and general impression. This is, of course, a very widespread impression. Peck and Havighurst (1960), for instance, suggest that if the school were the only agency for developing character, the result would be a morality built around a rather irrational conformity to rules and to authoritative impositions in general. They doubt that the school would be so effective in fostering the more responsible and more mature, but more risky, morality that comes from rational atruism.

Even if the teacher had clearly superior standing in the various aspects of the real-life curriculum, the school setting itself might stultify his tendency to present his subject in a real-life manner. Take sex, for instance. Suppose our teacher is well above average with respect to romantic competence, sexual decency, and other sexual attributes considered desirable. Can this teacher, however well-equipped, present sex topics in realistic, adult fashion? Can he discuss the topic as the students will hear it discussed outside the school, or as the typical parent will discuss it at the club or at a party? Or will our teacher be forced to present sheer biological information, giving the picture of a rather grim business of glands and secretions surrounded by alleged dangers of pregnancy and venereal disease? Can he show how sex operates in a complex social framework that is often more important than the basic physiology? Can he tell the student how to begin a flirtation, or, more important, perhaps, how to break it off? Yet in the real-life world these things may be more important than are the glands of Bartolini or the Vas deferens.

The possible worries about realistic sex education in the schools holds for other areas. Suppose that teachers actually do exemplify our ideals in the realms of surgent, gusty, goodnatured, spontaneous, social relations. There is still the danger that when these things become embalmed in the curriculum and communicated in the form of words and concepts we may still have a character that stresses logical considerations, and a pupil who regulates his social doings by chart and calendar, and who "does good" because of calculation and duty. Such studied morality, so suggestive of the prig, would be considered by many (Read, 1960) as the very antithesis of true character.

Possible Serious Neglect of the Academic

Our deductions from the sociological speculations in the theory of spontaneous schooling would lead us to fear that the school, in taking over major responsibility for real-life education, would produce results that would fail to satisfy many people. There is also a further danger: In taking on this additional obligation, the school may subject the traditional academic areas to unacceptable neglect.

From sheer common sense it would seem unlikely that a single institution can give impartial support both to matters that have urgent and immediate importance and to other matters that are important only occasionally and only in the long run. It might prove difficult, using an extreme example, for a single institution and a single administration to manage both a hospital and a museum. Any reasonable distribution of interest would give the lion's share of attention to the welfare of patients and only minor attention to statues and paintings. It would be difficult to maintain a balance in this matter. If the hospital were to secure adequate care, there is a danger that the museum may be neglected altogether. Clearly it would seem much better to place the responsibility for the museum in the hands of someone who in his day-by-day thoughts was deeply concerned about paintings and statuary. Such a person, in his more leisurely moments, of course, would admit that hospitals were more important. If he kept a record of his thoughts throughout the day, however, he would find them more concerned about lighting and varnishes than about fever charts and transfusions.

The hospital-museum analogy, farfetched as it is, has some application to the problem of personality versus (say) the role of the caesura in Virgil's poetry. Suppose the teacher of Latin is properly impressed about the relative long-range importance of a moderate amount of self-confidence as compared to a knowledge of the caesura. Suppose further that the teacher keeps the relative importance of these things clearly in his mind in his hour-by-hour teaching activities. Is there not a danger that the caesura will be neglected almost completely? It may be better for the teacher of Latin to admit frankly that self-confidence is more important than the caesura but at the same time to realize that the caesura is *his* job. Many other people, such as parents, friends, and club directors are interested in self-confidence, but if the Latin teacher does not teach the caesura, no one else will.

As character education becomes a more and more important part of the curriculum and as teachers come more and more to realize the overwhelming importance of character, we may find everyone tempted to rush off to these more important and interesting tasks and to neglect the less important and more prosaic academic tasks. Such a concentration of interest would have undesirable consequences if academic attainments are considered to have any importance at all. In our sociological speculations, of course, we have suggested that academic traits, although less crucial than character traits, have vast, residual importance. In the *long run,* indeed, our development in these traits may well decide whether we shall survive as a civilization or suffer extinction at the hands of some rival group.

Possibility of Two Separate Institutions

We are now in a bit of a quandary: The vital traits in the middle gradient must be nurtured. Their nurture constitutes an undeferrable demand. The urgent concern of parents, moreover, may be shrinking so much that it leaves this vital area uncared for. If the school moves into this neglected area, however, we face the risk of inadequate success. We also face the second risk of unacceptable neglect of the areas now nurtured by the school.

The most natural solution to this problem is the establishment of a separate agency or group of agencies dedicated to the furtherance of the vital areas. And, in connection with such crucial problems, some extra-school agency is frequently suggested either to replace or to supplement the school's efforts (Burchill, 1962; Dubos, 1961; Havighurst and Stiles, 1961; Lawhead, 1963; Mead, 1961). In mentioning these recent proposals, by the way, we do not wish to suggest that the general idea is novel. Church leaders for some years have held that true character cannot be adequately developed by secular schools.

All in all we may be expecting too much to hope that the pallid, but important, academic traits should flourish in cheek-by-jowl competition with the more robust vital traits of real life. When frail and unsubstantial concerns survive, it is usually through the intervention of some zealot who, for reasons of his own, sees great value in the perishable thing that he nurtures (see Chapter 10). It is some dedicated historical society that protects the antique building from the claims of the throughway. It is the zealous orchid fancier that champions his blooms in their unfair competition with more vigorous indigenous plants.

Society owes much to this champion of the offbeat and the perishable. True enough our champion is not always temperate in his insistences. Often he must be outvoted. But it is better to have an extreme advocate, destined to frequent defeat, than to trust to a dependable balance of interests existing within one mind. (This matter will be further discussed in Chapter 10.)

For these reasons it would seem better that the school should continue its traditional nurture of remote academic matters, and some less scholastic agencies be developed to provide the necessary nurture of the traits with immediate importance in real life.

In contrast to the school with its concern for the residual traits, this less academic institution or institutions, would be managed by people who are primarily concerned with the immediate demands of life as it is lived. They would act as professional parents, so to speak, and would labor to supply the necessary guidance in such vital areas as health, character, personal adjustment, and social responsibility. Naturally they would sympathize with the general objectives of the academician and would do what they could, in passing, to encourage proficiency in these matters. But in their hour-by-hour thoughts, the more vital curriculum would dominate.

In such a division of functions we would have the school managed by people who have exceptional concern for academic matters and who feel impelled to communicate with other people regarding those matters. These people would clearly realize that other activities had more immediate importance in the whole life of the child. They would recognize that in the entire scheme of things these academic matters constitute only one small part in the development of the whole child. They would recognize, moreover, that these academic matters must take second place to health, to happiness, and to social decency. But, having admitted these things, the members of the academic staff would still find their own thoughts chiefly occupied with academic development. Anxious to facilitate and encourage character development whenever they could, they would still devote the bulk of their time and energy to the academic matters which, were it not for them, would be completely neglected.

In a theoretical discussion such as this, it would seem unwise to provide a detailed blueprint of the less scholastic agencies to be given the responsibility for character education. The solution may lie in the simple process of giving more encouragement and more legal status to the many agencies now at work. Perhaps the churches, youth clubs, and various service organizations could do the job provided they were given much more support and provided each child were expected to associate himself with one agency or another. Perhaps, however, these should be supplemented by an institution under the direct control of some state agency.

As we leave the academic areas and move farther and farther into the more vital area of character, there is more and more justification for giving parents a more direct voice in the important decisions to be made. In the remote academic subjects the typical parent is not in a position to decide what is right and what is wrong. In dealing with character, however, the situation is quite different. Here crucial issues are at stake. And, within the broad limits of social decency, there is room for wide divergence of opinion as to approaches and as to ultimate metaphysical goals. In these areas, moreover, we cannot be sure that the layman must defer to the academic expert. Parents may be just as adequate as the typical schoolman in judging nobility, magnaminity, kindliness, or good sportsmanship.

As we move, then, from the academic realm to the area of character, we find that the expert loses some of his advantage in the matter of choosing goals and correct answers. He also loses some of his advantage in the matter of selecting competent people. Clearly if I am to decide whether or not Mr. Brown is qualified in algebra or geography it would be most helpful for me to know something of these subjects myself. And there is every justification for calling in the expert and the professional to judge the competence of teachers in these academic subjects.

But it does not always take a highly trained professional to judge such things as vigor, fairness, or steadfast dependability. Even in some areas of personal adjustment, the judgment of the reasonably informed layman may equal that of the expert. Undergraduates do as well as trained clinical psychologists in judging the mental hygiene significance of statements made by patients (Hunt and others, 1957). Grade teachers excel psychologists in predicting the things that children will approve or condemn (Goertzen, 1957). Specialized training in the interpretation of clinical symptoms has even led to reduced accuracy in this activity (Crow, 1957).

In promoting character and other aspects of real life, a relatively nonscholastic agency might have many advantages not ordinarily available to the school. An agency more directly involved in practical community affairs, for instance, would have a better opportunity for fostering in pupils the feeling of such involvement. And one of the traits of character needing to be developed is precisely this sense of intimate involvement in community, national, and international affairs (Lawhead, 1963). In many of these activities it would help if the student could regard himself as a responsible young adult and not as a legal infant or as a dependent—a role to which the status of student must tend to assign him. Lack of such a sense of involvement is in itself a defect in moral development. Through such a lack of commitment, moreover, a student becomes an easier prey to delinquency or aimless gang action. His feeling of not belonging to anything significant invites him to seek excitement and expression in other areas.

For these and for other practical reasons, there is much advocacy of work experience and for genuine community participation on the part of students of high school age (Burchill, 1962; Havighurst and Stiles, 1961). The more drastic proposals, naturally enough, are directed to the problems of delinquent or predelinquent students. The general idea of involving agencies and people outside the schools, however, is applicable to the entire area of developing responsible citizens (Dubos, 1961; Mead, 1961).

When it is difficult to provide genuine community participation, there may be some advantage in such watered-down aspects of real life as camping or in institutions as the old Civilian Conservation Corps organizations. Camping has been well regarded, and camping programs seem to be successful in aiding young people to become more responsible. That, at least, is the verdict of one unusually intensive scrutiny of the problem (Hyman and others, 1962), and of incidental reports (Bond, 1962).

Agencies outside the school might be freer to stress a sense of commitment that is not always open to the school. In the United States, particularly, the schools cannot readily link up with religious values. For this reason they may miss one powerful aid in bringing about a sense of commitment or of a purpose larger and more important than the individual himself. There are other types of commitments which, for one reason or another, are also less available to the school. Outside the school the young adult can be completely committed to one political party or to the economic fortunes of one company. The school, however, is less able to invoke such types of commitment.

Some of the general principles of learning also point to possible advantages of the nonscholastic agency, especially in dealing with the delinquent or near-delinquent. Consider, for instance, the principle of maintaining a schedule of success. The student tottering on the verge of delinquency will become more adequately socialized insofar as he can be led to make a succession of adequate reactions and isofar as he can be reinforced for each of those adequate reactions. To do this we wish to maximize his chances for early success. We should put him in some environment where, by good luck or good management, he will, some day, behave better than he is behaving today. At this point he should be led to experience genuine reinforcement. It is an open question if the predelinquent feels a marked glow from the approval of the typical teacher. On the contrary, in order to survive, he has often had to write off that kind of approval as unimportant.

When we think of conditions which favor success, we must realize that the school may not be our best hope for the delinquent. It is not the environment in which he is most likely to put his best foot forward. For the near-delinquent, the school is the epitome of the difficult environments with which he must contend. Rejection of the school and all that it stands for is one of the most typical characteristics of the delinquent. For him, failure in scholastic tasks is the rule.

In attempting to get more adequate social behavior from the delinquent or predelinquent, the school clearly faces a serious problem in transfer. Decent behavior within the school, of course, is important in its own right. But our most important problem is to get him to behave better in real life. If, in spite of the odds against us, we socialize him within the school, we must still depend on tremendous transfer if we hope for an improvement outside the school. It would seem better to have him learn this more reasonable behavior in a situation that more closely resembled real life and in one which permitted greater likelihood of early success.

All in all, the theory of spontaneous schooling would suggest that the school faces more risk of failure as it moves into the areas of character education. In view of that likelihood of failure, it might be wise to examine the powers of other agencies in cultivating this most important area.

REFERENCES

Bond, Marjorie, H., Teenage attitudes and attitude change as measured by the Q-technique, *J. educ. Sociol.*, 1962, *36*, 10–19.

Burchill, G. W., *Work-study programs for alienated youth, a casebook*. Chicago: Science Research Associates, 1962.

Coslin, F., and W. D. Kerr, The effects of an abnormal psychology course on students' attitudes toward mental illness, *J. educ. Psychol.*, 1962, *53*, 214–218.

Crow, W. J., The effect of training upon accuracy and variability in interpersonal perception, *J. abnorm. soc. Psychol.*, 1957, *55*, 355–359.

Dell, G. A., Social factors and school influence in juvenile delinquency, *Brit. J. educ. Psychol.*, 1963, *33*, 312–322.

Dubos, R. J., Adaptability for survival and growth, in E. Ginzberg, ed., *Values and ideals of American youth*. New York: Columbia University Press, 1961, 3–13.

Freedman, M. B., *Impact of college, new dimensions in higher education*. Washington, D.C.: U.S. Government Printing Office, 1960, No. 4.

Goertzen, S. M., A study of teachers' and psychologists' ability to predict seventh graders' opinions of certain behaviors of their peer group, *J. educ. Psychol.*, 1957, *48*, 166–170.

Havighurst, R. J., and L. J. Stiles, National policy for alienated youth, *Phi Delta Kappan*, 1961, *42*, 283–291.

Hovland, C. I., Yale studies of communication and persuasion, in W. W. Charters, Jr., and N. L. Gage, eds., *Readings in the social psychology of education*. Boston: Allyn and Bacon, 1963, 239–253.

Hunt, W. A., N. F. Jones, and E. B. Hunt, Reliability of clinical judgments as a function of clinical experience, *J. clin. Psychol.*, 1957, *13*, 377–379.

Hyman, H. H., C. R. Wright, and T. K. Hopkins, *Applications of methods of evaluation: four studies of the encampment for citizenship*. Berkeley, Calif.: University of California Press, 1962.

Jacob, P. E., *Changing values in college: an exploratory study of the impact of college teaching*. New York: Harper & Row, 1957.

Jones, H. E., The longitudinal method in the study of personality, in I. Iscoe and H. W. Stevenson, eds., *Personality development in children*. Austin, Tex.: University of Texas Press, 1960, 3–27.

Jones, V., Character education, *Encyclopaedia of Educational Research*, second ed. New York: Macmillan, 1960, 184–191.

Jones, V., Character development in children—an objective approach, in L. Carmichael, ed., *Manual of child psychology*, second ed. New York: Wiley, 1954, 781–832.

Kraus, S., Modifying prejudice: attitude change as a function of the race of the communicator, *Audiovis. Commun. Rev.*, 1962, *10*, 14–22.

Lawhead, V. B., A curriculum for citizenship education, in A. Frazier, ed., *New insights and the curriculum, Yearb. Ass. Superv. and Curric. Develpm.* Washington, D.C.: NEA, 1963, 263–282.

Lichtenstein, A. *Can attitudes be taught?* Johns Hopkins University Studies in Education, No. 21, 1934.

McClintock, C. G., and H. A. Turner, The impact of college upon political knowledge, participation, and values, *Hum. Relat.*, 1962, *15*, 165–176.

McCord, W., and Joan McCord, *Origins of crime: a new evaluation of the Cambridge-Somerville youth study.* New York: Columbia University Press, 1959.

Mead, Margaret, The young adult, in E. Ginzberg, ed., *Values and ideals of American youth.* New York: Columbia University Press, 1961, 37–51.

Merril, I. R., Attitude films and attitude change, *Audiovis. Commun. Rev.*, 1962, *10*, 3–13.

Murphy, Lois B., *The widening world of childhood.* New York: Basic Books, 1962.

Peck, R. F., and R. J. Havighurst, *The psychology of character development.* New York: Wiley, 1960.

Peterson, Ruth C., and L. L. Thurstone, *Motion pictures and the social attitudes of children.* New York: Macmillan, 1933.

Plant, W. T., Changes in ethnocentrism associated with a four-year college education, *J. educ. Psychol.*, 1959, *49*, 162–165.

Read, Sir Herbert, Esthetics: enemy of violence? *Saturday Rev.*, 1960 (Dec. 4), *43*, No. 52, 9–11.

Stember, C. H., *Education and attitude change: the effect of schooling on prejudice against minority groups.* New York: Institute of Human Relations Press, 1961.

Tait, C. D., Jr., and E. F. Hodges, Jr., *Delinquents, their families and the community.* Springfield, Ill.: Charles C Thomas, 1962.

Webster, H., M. Freedman, and P. Heist, Personality changes in college students, in N. Sanford, ed., *The American college.* New York: Wiley, 1962, 811–846.

Weltman, Naomi, and H. H. Remmers, Pupils', parents' and teachers' attitudes—similarities and differences, *Purdue Univ. Stud. higher Educ.*, 1946, *56*, 1–52.

Young, R. K., W. M. Benson, and W. H. Holtzman, Change in attitudes toward the Negro in a southern university, *J. abnorm. soc. Psychol.*, 1960, *60*, 131–133.

10 | SOME SALUTARY IRONIES AND THE CONSOLATIONS THEY PROVIDE

If we should be cautious in drawing implications from the serious psychological aspects of the theory, we should be even more circumspect in making deductions from our speculations about the historical origins of the schools. It happens, however, that the theory of the social functions of the school, if it can be verified, would provide a fairly complete explanation of two interesting, if distressing, phenomena of schooling, and these should be examined. I refer, first, to the niggardly support often given to the schools in the face of great verbal approval and, second, to the problem of academic snobbery, or the tendency of the academician to venerate the esoteric or precious at the expense of the practical or vital. Both of these phenomena become more understandable, although perhaps no more palatable, in the light of the sociological speculations advanced by the theory.

Every society has to deal with things which are not continuously important but which are of tremendous importance on those few occasions when they are needed. The fire engine in a modern small community, for instance, may be needed very infrequently. When it is needed, however, it is most important that it be in working order. The army of a peaceful country likewise may be superfluous most of the time, but it is of vital significance that it should be ready on those rare occasions when it is needed.

According to the sociological speculations advanced in Chapter 3, the tendencies nurtured by the school have little immediate, continuous importance but have an importance that is remote and sporadic. These activities also require dedicated attention during those long periods when they lack immediate and obvious importance.

Such remote and sporadic concerns require a special kind of support. It is easy to summon aid when the fire is in progress but not so easy to enlist volunteers to keep the fire house tidy. It is easy to get legislators to allocate money to correct a worrisome academic deficiency in our young adults but more difficult to summon the aid which will nourish abilities not yet in demand.

The support required for these activities has another characteristic: it must not be overdone. If we were too successful in persuading people to tidy up the firehouse, more vital concerns might suffer. And if all our energy were expended by our support of the esoteric concerns of the school, our whole society might perish. This latter problem may not worry us so much in these days of abundant energy, but it was probably a serious issue during the days that our social institutions were evolving. During those days, the earthy mechanisms needed to provide support for schooling must have been coupled with other mechanisms, equally earthy, to prevent schooling from being carried to an unwholesome excess.

As one device for supporting these activities with remote or sporadic survival value, many individuals or groups have employed powerful sanctions, the sanctions becoming more and more vigorous as the matters involved become more easy to neglect. Knowing his proneness to forget the church, the devout man may set up a procedure whereby duty to the church must be performed before other activities are permitted. Aware of his tendency to waste his money, the careful man may set aside a sum for the savings bank before he permits himself to spend any of his earnings. In many other areas we may see unusual sanctions or rituals attached to institutions, such as marriage or social convention, and such sanctions may constitute a device for providing these somewhat precarious institutions with artificial support.

Specialized Agencies

Another device, by no means inconsistent with the first, is the utilization of some special agency for the care of the activity likely to be neglected. The priest, for instance, may be encouraged to remind us of our spiritual status. The budget officer may be installed to remind us of the dangers of profligacy. Peacetime army officers may be retained for the precise purpose of keeping the army at a high level of efficiency in the very days when it has no genuine function to perform.

Presumably, societies in many regions and in many eras have profited from the dedication of special groups keenly interested in esoteric or unusual matters. It is not to be suggested, however, that societies have deliberately arranged for these helpful activities. It is more likely, that such interests and their dedicated cheering sections developed spontaneously, and the total society has merely been the unknowing beneficiary of the effects produced. It is also assumed, moreover, that, in their unconscious exploitation of these useful zealots, most societies offered a form of support that was also largely automatic and spontaneous.

The support provided by these devices becomes more pronounced as we approach the areas that have little immediate or primitive survival value in their own right. We spend little time in reminding people that they should breathe. We need no organized cheering section to remind physicians of the importance of their work. Until recently, at least, there have been few organized societies to urge us to earn money or to seek the favors of the opposite sex. The affairs that need and get continual verbal support are the esoteric matters with remote survival value. Conversely, when we find a group of dedicated champions consistently preaching the importance of thrift, of further education, of disinterested research, we can suspect that these powerful sanctions are a tribute not to the immediate importance of the activities but to their frailty and to their inability to survive without the special sanctions. In observing the special care lavished upon the weakling in the family, for instance, we should not conclude that he is intrinsically more important than the others but merely that he has comparable importance, and without the special concern, he would not survive at all. In hearing the claims of Latin exalted and the virtues of typing derogated, we should not conclude that Latin is fundamentally more important, but merely it is less vigorous; without this dedicated support, it could not contend with the more vital and robust concerns that press upon us with more immediate insistence.

Some Consequences of Utilizing the Dedicated Specialist

It would not be surprising that surviving societies have frequently stumbled upon the device of exploiting the zealot to guarantee some development of the offbeat matters with remote and sporadic importance.

The unconscious use of this readily available resource offers an economy that could hardly have been neglected. But the efficient utilization of this specialist also presents some problems. For one thing, he must be supported. At certain points, moreover, he must be restrained.

Need for Support

Any society should provide a special kind of support to get reasonable returns from those dedicated to esoteric activities. To keep the devotee at work, the other members of the group should confirm his conviction of the importance of his work. Even if his supporters, for instance, suspected in their own minds that his usefulness lay chiefly in the problematic future, they should never advance their suspicions to him. It is far better to give verbal assent to his insistence that the things with which he deals are eternally important, day in and day out.

When the esoteric activities are of an abstract or immaterial nature, there arises a special need for support. Such dealing with the abstract seldom brings about the immediate feedback that is found in many practical affairs. In more earthy enterprises, the moment-by-moment significance of one's acts are often immediately and forcefully apparent. The burned food calls attention to itself. The awkward social gesture brings its own rebuff. The neglect of a ritual, however, or a mistake in reading the stars may have no such drastic or obvious consequences. Lacking concrete evidence that his doings are significant, the dealer in the abstract or spiritual requires much verbal reassurance and must be encouraged frequently and generously by those around him. Lavish verbal support is often the rule for activities that have chiefly remote survival value.

Although the true zealot needs conviction, and although he flourishes under generous verbal support, he will often do quite well with only limited practical support. For him, lip service may suffice. The antiquarian, the artist, and the clergyman, when convinced of the importance of their work, may continue their efforts under appalling practical neglect.

In this, it will be noted, we have a clear-cut invitation to hypocrisy. Survival circumstances have insisted that we provide lip service. These same circumstances, however, have not insisted that we provide practical support commensurate with our verbal protestation. In this situation we are likely to find a discrepancy between word and action. This will be dealt with later.

Need for Restraint

To exploit the dedicated specialist, a surviving society should have stumbled upon some way of giving the special kind of support that he requires. But it must also have stumbled upon some devices for keeping him within bounds.

The concerns nurtured by the zealot, after all, do not have the highest priority in their demands for support. True, they must not be completely neglected, but neither must they dominate. If, at any moment, there is not enough support to go around, the claims of schooling must stand aside until the more immediate or primitive areas have been supported. The museum must remain in darkness until there is more than enough emergency lighting for the operating room. A subtle balance is required in these matters, something similar to a reasonable balance between the claims of one's livelihood, on the one hand, and the claims of one's hobby or recreation, on the other. The man who seriously neglects his livelihood for golf may promptly lose out. In the longer run, however, the man who completely neglects his recreation may also lose out. The most favorable arrangement is seen in the man who permits vital interests to dominate but who allows a measure of interest for matters with more remote and problematic return.

Clearly this favorable balance of support is likely to be destroyed if the zealot is allowed to go as far as he chooses. Convinced of the tremendous and continuous importance of his interests, he could, if we let him, bleed us white in building the edifice to which he is dedicated, in supporting the crusade which his zeal sees as necessary, or in maintaining the research project in which he finds vast intellectual excitement. To a Tsar Lazaar, completely devoted to the claims of the spirit, it is more important to cleanse the soul of its impurities than to repel the enemy attack. This may be the way to ultimate spiritual grace but it does not promote immediate survival of the group in question. We need an extremely dedicated and jealous champion to permit the weakling among our concerns to survive at all. The eager support of the weakling, however, if carried too far, could work to the detriment of the more robust concerns and of society at large.

How, then, can we make use of the partisan's zeal and, at the same time, restrain him, yet, in restraining him, not undo him? In many of the laments so frequently uttered, one can detect the hope that the zealot would manage all this within himself. In the zealot that we exploit, we would also like to find the completely judicious man. This angelic creature would have a just appreciation of the importance of his own cherished enterprises but would see the claims of those enterprises in relation to the demands of other activities. He would ask only for what he needed and would be prepared to temper his demands if the more vital activities should suffer.

We seem completely unrealistic in this yearning for the completely judicious man or for a profession composed of such judicious men. Similarly in the law courts, it has seemed unrealistic to hope for a group of men completely dedicated to determining the objective truth. It has seemed much safer to rely on the motivations inherent in the adversary system, where the excesses of one man's efforts have a chance of being counterbalanced by the avowed partisanship of his opponent. In this adversary system, society utilizes the motivation of people who, unrestrained, would go too far. Most societies have thus worked out the necessary restraints. To get a horse that will go fast enough, we get one who will try to go too fast, and then we rein him in. To get a man who will do enough for academic subjects, we get a man who will try to do too much, and then we subject him to the necessary constraints. In doing this, we condemn him to a life of frustration. It will be his destiny always to try and frequently to fail. This frustration is a price he must pay to carry on his important survival task.

At times the restraint applied is of a sporadic and precipitous nature. During a long period, the scholastic zealot is given his head. Then suddenly, violently, he is pulled up short. The philosopher is permitted, and encouraged, to hold forth up to a point, but when his influence becomes so pronounced that there seems to be danger of corrupting the youth, a Socrates is put to death. The religious order may work for centuries in its own quiet way, but when its influence becomes excessive, a prominent order, such as the Jesuits, may find itself expelled from the nation.

Compared to an unrealistic hope of self-restraint, and compared to a sporadic, sudden and punitive restriction, there is much to be said for the natural and steady control that lies in the inevitable discrepancy between word and deed. As we have pointed out, circumstances invite us to provide less practical support than our verbal protestations would imply. Going farther, survival conditions almost demand that we practice this saving hypocrisy. Verbally we must spur the zealot on. Practically we rein him in.

This beneficent double-dealing, like most survival-favoring devices, is not something that we have to strive hard to acquire. It is a device that most people employ without thinking or without effort. In the presence of the teacher or scholar, both student and alumnus praise the world of books and ideas. As the door closes behind him, however, the youth returns to venery and good-fellowship, and his elders return to business, politics, and golf. In the legislature everyone speaks for more and better education, but the voting record may tell a different story. The pastor is piously assured of the supreme importance of his work. When he asks for a contribution to match this assurance, however, he is reminded of the necessity of being reasonable in these matters.

This unlovely discrepancy between word and deed, then, is to be seen, not as gratuitous malice, but as a survival-favoring device which has evolved as a means of balancing the necessary support of schools with the necessary controls that prevent us from becoming dangerously scholar-ridden. This inconsistency between protestation and performance, with all its distressing features, seems a far better means of providing the salutary restraint than any alternative that has so far appeared.

Better, that is to say, so long as it works. But there may be a danger that this useful hypocrisy is about to lose its effectiveness. Like many other survival devices, this discrepancy between word and deed is not pretty, nor superficially defensible. With increasing exposure, this unesthetic device may wither away. And one seems to detect in the youth of today less tolerance for such inconsistency. For good or for ill, the modern youth is less than happy when expected to profess democracy but to practice discrimination. He experiences no mere indulgent amusement at the discrepancy between camp-meeting avowal of virtue and the after-meeting activities in the woods. The furtive delights of stolen fruits are not for him. The modern college student has no taste for the clandestine sexual encounters that so entranced his father. Instead he insists that the adult world look on, and applaud, or certainly approve, while he boldly escorts his paramour to the dormitory room. If an activity is to be carried on, it must also be granted verbal approval. Conversely, if we supply verbal support, we must, on Monday morning, come across with the last implication of our Sunday protestations.

If this distaste for a sophisticated insincerity should become the rule, we would expect the society in question to be in for trouble. Either it would have to keep its verbal support at moderate, and perhaps ineffective, levels or it would have to provide a practical support for schools and similar enterprises that would endanger the earthy concerns vital to group survival.

The Phenomenon of Academic Snobbery

The specialized concerns of the schoolman or academician constitute one agency that neatly supplements the interests and compulsions of other agencies such as the family. Looking at the specialized interests of the academician from the outside and regarding them as one undifferentiated group of interests, we have seen how these interests and concerns can be spontaneously utilized by the host group. We have also seen how these intense concerns must be contained if they are to be kept from harming the more vital areas of life.

Within the realm of academic interests, there must be a pattern geared to the decline of the support received from society as a whole. As the general support falls off, the specialized academic support must rise to make good the deficit. The support provided by the school must be the mirror image of the support coming from other agencies. Typing, being important in a practical way, can get along with the indulgent toleration of the schools. Ancient History, having little practical promise, requires consistent and solicitous support.

It is the established academician or schoolman, of course, who must provide this pattern. Presumably he could discharge his obligations by making deliberate rational decisions. Seeing that the general support of society is sinking, he could deliberately increase the intensity of his own concerns. Noting that other agencies have moved in to care for some other area, he could now reduce his concern to a more relaxed and indulgent level.

But this would surely be an undependable device! Things would be managed much more effectively if the established academician were moved chiefly by built-in concerns. If he is to be effective he cannot see his educational values as merely supplementing the values of other agencies. He should be driven by the salutary illusion that his values are the real values; that Latin *has* a higher claim than typing; that research into exotic matters *is* more worthwhile than research into the practical.

Not only does the true academician feel that he can ignore the more practical things; he must go much farther. Being so constituted as to nourish the exotic, he actually feels hostility and contempt for the more prosaic items about to invade his camp. Similarly, the nurturer of a rare and delicate plant would be up in arms if he saw some more robust and more immediately useful vegetable about to intrude.

It is this salutary illusion, of course, that constitutes the academic snobbery we have set out to explain. Here it is seen as an almost inevitable result of the basic forces held to be responsible for schooling in the first place. Although we may seek to alter these perversities, we should spend little time in merely bewailing them. In utilizing the zealot we must expect his excesses.

Taking the long-range view, we can easily see these academic excesses as inevitable and generally useful, even if slightly weird and amusing. But not everyone is in a position to enjoy this long-range view. The student immersed in the system can seldom see the total survival picture and the part in it that his schooling plays. He cannot regard these academic emphases or perversities primarily as interesting foibles inherent in a valuable sociological mechanism. For him, on the contrary, these emphases or perversities are the inescapable realities with which he must contend each day. The same situation applies to the young man just becoming established in the academic profession. Like the student, he is not likely to see these academic emphases in their broad perspective. For him they constitute the grim realities that determine his success or failure. And any apparent inversion in these controlling values is likely to induce serious distress.

Containing the Academic Excesses

In spite of the very definite long-range value in the academician's stress on the esoteric, society may well see the need for some restraint. Like any other arrangement predicated on excess, this pressure, if unhindered, might go too far. And even in university circles there has been much worry (Bartlett, 1947) over the tendency to exalt the intellect to an inordinate extent, and to disparage more primitive concerns.

Until recently, academic excesses have been held in check by many effective counterforces. Any undue exaltation of esoteric and intellectual matters would be promptly offset by the vigorous claims of food, of sex, of companionship, of worldly gain, and of the joys of social power. In the past these things would press so powerfully that they should prevent any academic reversal of values from prevailing in any complete fashion.

In the past, any excessive influence of the academic has also been offset to some extent by the very image of the teacher and professor. In the typical stereotype, the scholar is underpaid, absent-minded, and remote from practical influence. Everything about him suggested that his values prevailed in a special world, far different from the real world that the student expected to inhabit.

Just as the teacher was dismissed in indulgent and patronizing fashion so the whole institution of schooling was considered to belong to the world of childhood, a world quite remote from the intense interests of men of affairs. Just as the child would emerge from the nursery, so the adolescent would soon leave the realm of the unwordly academician and move into the world of men. True, the very rare youth would continue his association with the academician even into early adulthood. Upon his return from the ivy halls, however, such a one would experience a very definite confrontation with the real world. This real world, only slighly contaminated by academic excesses, should provide a healthy corrective.

But things may now be changing so much that the historical counter-forces no longer serve. For one thing, the claims of many earthy concerns may no longer press upon us quite so harshly. In many regions, for instance, hunger is not a serious problem. For another thing, the public image of the scholar may now be changing, and he may now appear more and more as a man of affairs. And although his affluence may be less than has been suggested, we find the top positions of the scholastic world to be very lucrative, indeed, lucrative enough to attract the attention of the economic man. Insofar as the scholar has now become a man of substance, his concerns are less likely to be dismissed with an indulgent smile. These concerns may seem to attain an importance comparable to the more earthy activities of the businessman or manufacturer.

If, as earlier suggested, there is an increasing need to reconcile word and action, this might also lead the student to carry into real life the attitudes he had professed in the classroom, even when those attitudes represent an unrealistic excess.

Finally, the sheer increase in the number of man-years of exposure to education may result in the greater and greater acceptance of all the values, however extreme, that are stressed in the school. At one time, only the occasional youth remained in the schools into his manhood years. Upon his return to his native community this potential scholar would soon become apprised of any academic excesses. Now, however, if the whole community is similarly exposed, there will be less likelihood of such a useful confrontation.

So runs the argument. If schools did arise largely from the natural operation of the postulated spontaneous tendencies, we would expect, though not necessarily welcome, these seeming paradoxes that so often distress us. To provide nurture for the tendencies with remote and sporadic value, it is most natural that societies should unconsciously rely on the built-in zeal of the specialist. But to do this is inevitably to invite the very excesses that we may deplore.

Stripped of their context, these excesses always strike us as paradoxical. Sometimes they do no more than that. When the excesses take the form of academic snobbery, for instance, we can often view them as amusing but harmless perversities. At other times, however, we cannot be so indulgent. When these same excesses pose a serious threat to more vital concerns, a surviving society must invoke effective restraints. One of the most natural, spontaneous restraints is to deny with the right hand what seems to be promised by the left.

In the light of the spontaneous forces, speculatively advanced to account for the origin of the schools, this unsavory ambivalence toward education appears as a valuable survival agency. Looking to the future, our fears should be not that this hypocrisy may persist, but, on the contrary, that this historical and salutary restraint may lose its force. If legislatures do come to suit their actions to their words, or if an undue proportion of our populace should become completely committed as adults to the more extreme academic values espoused as students, then perhaps some supplementary restraint or corrective may be necessary to bring home to our youth Gardner's (1961) warning that plumbing has its heroes nothing less than art.

REFERENCES

Bartlett, F. C., The twentieth Maudsley lecture: intelligence as a social problem, *J. ment. Sci.*, 1947, *93*, 1–8.
Gardner, J. W., Excellence, can we be equal and excellent too? New York: Harper & Row, 1961.

11 | PRESCRIPTION FOR RELAXATION

If the theory of spontaneous schooling should be validated, or partly validated, it would, true enough, confirm us in our current belief that schools are vitally important. In the same breath, however, the theory would invite us to adopt a relaxed and confident attitude toward the process of schooling, however vital. In dealing with schooling, as in dealing with so many other vital processes, we are reminded that we can rely on powerful, pervasive forces, ready to do their work with only moderate deliberate direction from us.

In dealing with crucial problems, of course, the most convincing reassurance comes from the awareness of the built-in machinery that can be depended upon to take care of matters. Apart from hemophiliacs, for instance, few people even think of the danger of bleeding to death when they notice the cut finger. But the spontaneous theory offers further reassurance. It also points to the simple and acceptable deliberate remedies that are available if necessary. At times, moreover, the spontaneous theory enables us to see that an apparent menace is really nothing more than a semantic problem. Described in terms of more basic forces, the menace turns out to be no problem at all. Finally the theory suggests the inevitability of minor imperfections in the broad beneficent pattern of schooling. And thus, in absolving us of blame, the theory should enable us to contemplate those imperfections with greater equanimity.

Consider a hypothetical school representing the ultimate in educational impoverishment. Suppose that a community, hitherto devoid of schools, has just made a crude beginning. By some rough and ready means, the community has been able to select a few people who, first of all, are proficient in the concerns that other people venerate but neglect, and who, secondly, are communicative by nature. The community has also made some arrangement, or has utilized some arrangement, whereby children regularly spend a portion of their time in close association with the people thus selected.

In presenting this illustration, it may be noted, we have ignored the speculative, sociological aspects of our theory. According to these sociological speculations, the community would not have to take any deliberate steps to assemble the "teachers," or to arrange for their association with children. These things would come about automatically. In this immediate discussion, however, we are concerned not with the origin of the schools, but with the confidence we can feel about the efficacy of schools once they are established.

From such a minimal school, however established, what could we confidently expect in the way of acceptable schooling?

The Adequacy of the Resulting Curriculum

With the primitive school thus established, the rest of us could confidently go our own way, being reassured that our residual concerns are receiving some attention. The *de facto*, or working, curriculum of this school is built upon no house of sand. It is not at the mercy of a teacher who grimly, but precariously, forces himself into surly compliance with an artificial curriculum imposed from above. Our curriculum stems, instead, from the built-in concerns for which the teachers have been selected. Rather than enforced compliance, we have a natural, almost compulsive, expression of the lively concerns at work within the teaching staff.

There is, of course, a price we must pay for this happy state of affairs. We must be reconciled to the approximate nature of that curriculum. It would be unrealistic to expect that this vital unwritten curriculum, arising not from precise words but from urgent natural concerns, would neatly reflect everything that each of us would like the schools to do. It would be necessary, on the contrary, to be content with something which, in the long run, and on the average, would roughly approximate the general concerns of most people.

In reconciling ourselves to the approximate nature of this curriculum, it might help to realize that such an approximation is not only acceptable but inevitable. Any more formal curriculum that we may contrive, with whatever agony of decision and redecision, will have to operate through the interests, natural or acquired, which direct the teacher's moment-by-moment interaction with his pupils. It is true, of course, that a more carefully formulated curriculum might, by one means or another, shape this pattern of effective interests. But even the most precise instrument must work through the interests to which the teacher, gladly or grudgingly, gives expression. And under these circumstances we cannot expect that the interests as expressed will neatly correspond to the hopes of those who phrased the elaborate document now reposing in the teacher's desk.

In facing the approximate nature of this, or any, curriculum, we might find further solace in the fact that, in any case, no one can predict the very best curriculum for the schools. Of all the residual concerns now being entertained, which have the most pronounced claim for expression? Who can tell? Which of these concerns, if continuously expressed within the classroom, would do most to help our children live richer lives at the moment? Which, in turn, would help them to cope with the problems they will face as adults? Which concerns, if cultivated over the centuries, would enable our descendants to deal with the unforeseen problems of those times? Here we face vast uncertainty at every step. We are about to throw a bottled message into the sea and to entrust it to the whims of the tides and the winds. Why strain for undue precision in the manner in which we take aim and throw? Almost any set of residual concerns, consistently expressed, carries some promise of useful results. It is hard to see in any precise fashion that any one set has much more warrant than another.

In thus advocating a dependence on the shot-gun factor in the curriculum, we are clearly questioning the value of logic or rationality in these important educational decisions. In respect to the curriculum as in so many respects, the theory of spontaneous schooling would place only minor faith in logic or rationality as the determiners of educational decisions or outcomes. In the view here presented, the primitive forces will continue to produce schooling, whether accompanied by a valid rationale, by a phony rationale, or by no rationale at all. Like the phenomena of love and courtship, the phenomena of schooling often show a blithe indifference to considerations of logic or rationality. With impeccable argument, for instance, you persuade some parent that the junior college is the proper place for his son. You show him that the two years in this program constitute the bulk of general education, or it can be used to provide a reasonable vocational training. Your listener gives verbal assent to every point you make, and, then promptly strains every resource to send his son to a four-year college.

The drive for a college education is a good illustration of the limitations of rational considerations. To make college or other schooling attractive or acceptable, societies have not been able to depend on logical argument, but have had to resort to more powerful and arbitrary weapons such as those of scorn and contempt. We wither under the charge of being uneducated, whether or not there is any logical need that we should be educated. However irrelevant or inconsequential the incident, we blush, and our friends blush for us, when some slip, some exhibition of irrelevant ignorance, lays us open to the charge of being an uneducated person. This quasi-snob aspect of education is most clearly seen in England where mere accent is often the passport to acceptance. But in any culture there are many shibboleths that must be honored by anyone who would escape the contempt or disregard which the uneducated often feel to be their lot.

When acted on by such irrational pressures, the great drive is not for genuine learning or self-improvement, but to be recognized and accepted as an educated person. If the current badge to such acceptance is a dueling scar, an approved accent, or a degree from an ivy-league college, that is what we seek. We may give logical assent to the argument that the junior college provides all that we need, or that the English "secondary modern" school has the curriculum which is a better answer to our needs. But having given this assent, the American student seeks a four-year college, and the English parent hopes that his children will make it to the "grammar" school.

Separation of Home and School

After setting up the primitive school, our community is seen as going blithely on its way and leaving the school to manage its own affairs. The community, of course, provides the necessary support, both physical and moral. But there is no suggestion that it goes in for the frantic cooperation between home and school that is so often advocated at present.

Would it be safe or permissible for the community to adopt this confident and relaxed attitude, and to feel that the school could safely be left to go its own way? It is, perhaps, no answer to this question to say that, whatever the frantic protestations to the contrary, this is actually what we do today. There is some consolation however, in the argument that such a separation is inevitable. More important, we suggest that the fancied evils of the separation are not as serious as they have been made to seem.

According to the broader aspects of the theory, we might well be skeptical about any great success in coordinating the school and the home. The chief reason for the school's existence in the first place, is held to lie in the home's lack of urgent, continual interest in the tasks undertaken by the school. In unconsciously or spontaneously developing schools to take care of this problem, societies have evolved a most useful arrangement, and it is questionable if this separation of responsibility should be lightly done away with. At any rate, any attempt to provide intimate coordination of the school and the home would seem to be working against nature. In the vast majority of homes, the typical parent feels only a long-range, indulgent interest in the welfare of the schools, and is quite glad to delegate detailed responsibility to the people in the profession. Very often any more intimate interest on the part of parents is brought about by appeals to parental sense of duty, by incidental enticements, and by outright pressure exerted through the shrill demands of children who plead to have their class represented at parent-teacher meetings.

It is true, of course, that in some middle-class communities, obtrusive interest in the schools has reached a fever pitch, and parents are never done running to the schools to participate in the training of their children. Under these circumstances, however, the other party to the coordination would often welcome a decrease in fervor. Many a teacher in these communities must wish that parents had something else to do.

What happens to the child if such coordination or integration is lacking? If the child should grow up in an environment that is not integrated, will he become a disintegrated individual? Surely not. He has facilities for integrating or dealing with diverse experiences, just as he has facilities for integrating diverse nutriments. And *he* must do it. Even if we fed him a predigested bolus, he would still have much integrating to do. Who of us, by the way, would welcome some such pseudo-omniscient coordination of our own experiences? Would we not feel that the world was ganging up on us in intolerable fashion if some superagency made sure that our experiences in the cocktail lounge were always consistent with our experiences at home, on the camping trip, or in church?

Educational Growth: Normal but Not Guaranteed

The view here put forward invites a relaxed attitude toward educational growth. Under very ordinary circumstances a moderate amount of educational growth is quite likely to occur. The growth that takes place under the eye of the teacher is not like the development of some hot-house plant which will perish if we make one false move. It is, on the contrary, a very robust, resilient growth which will often continue in the face of adverse circumstances. In this respect, scholastic growth is held to resemble the physical growth of the child. In the latter area we can expect that with any one of a large number of diets a reasonable amount of physical growth will take place. We can expect, also, that a change from an extremely poor diet or regimen will lead to a perceptible, but slight, improvement in physical growth. We know, too, that the adoption of a "super" regimen cannot be expected to produce corresponding changes in physical stature.

But in scholastic growth, as in physical growth, we must be prepared for unhappy exceptions. Under these or any other provisions, there are bound to be pupils who fail to profit from the regular experience that suffices for most people. In any system this fact should be faced and openly dealt with.

In the face of this inescapable fact, how can we justify our dependence on the very ordinary facilities suggested? Do we, in effect, disregard the claims of those who may fall by the wayside? By no means! Here again we return to the parallel problem of health and physical growth. As we have stated, the general rough and ready dietary program provided by the ordinary mother will insure reasonable physical growth and reasonable health for *most* children. But there are bound to be some children for whom this homespun regimen will not work. And, when a child fails to respond to the general routine, an expert is called in.

In discussing the staffing of the schools we again invoke the nutritional analogy, and ask that an expert be available to deal with these inevitable educational deficiencies. It seems more sensible to provide the occasional services of the expert than to insist, unrealistically, that every teacher be capable of preventing these lapses, or to insist, uneconomically, that every teacher be sufficiently trained to deal with these lapses once they do occur.

Less Anxiety about Staffing the Schools

According to our theory, there should be a vast pool of talent for teaching, distributed throughout the general population. The basic mechanisms responsible for teaching reside in some very earthy, primitive tendencies. Although more pronounced in some people than in others, these tendencies are quite prevalent. In a great many people we should find the potential which, if suitably developed, should result in acceptable teaching.

This prevalence of teaching aptitude is periodically exploited by the military. When the military training centers must be expanded rapidly, teachers are often created by sheer fiat. Men are drawn out of the ranks almost at random and told to instruct. This, of course, does not always result in inspired teaching, but it does fairly regularly result in some learning on the part of the pupils, even on the part of pupils whose appetite for learning is no greater than the urge of the teacher who has been ordered to instruct.

Our theory asks that teachers clearly exceed the general population in their interest and mastery of academic subjects and in their various communicative compulsions. They must be also inclined, or induced, to associate with pupils.

Much educational growth is held to stem from the school's reputation as a conservator of academic values (Chapter 5). For this reason, our theory asks that teachers not only have superior knowledge of academic matters, but that they should also have a reputation for such knowledge. They should be able to symbolize the things for which the school stands. The teacher in any community should be regarded in that community as an educated person. He should certainly be so regarded by an articulate elite having a pronounced influence on general community views.

When nothing better offered, this reputation for scholarship might serve as one basis for selecting teachers. The typical man in the street, for instance, could ordinarily list two or three of his acquaintances whom he considers to have more than average knowledge of history, astronomy, or other academic subjects. These acquaintances, in turn, could name other people knowing even more about the academic subjects than he does. At the second or third stage of such nominations, we might reach a fairly dependable consensus indicating academic competence.

Keeping in mind the large pool of moderate talent, we can conceive of an educational system based on different degrees of professionalization. In this system, the basic "teachers" consist of a group of younger people, reasonably competent in the subject matter for which they are responsible, and moved to communicate with the students under their care, but falling far short of the paragons so often described in the starry-eyed, recruitment pamphlets, and so seldom encountered in these earthly regions.

According to our theory we should in no way be frightened by the prospect of such basic teachers, subject to frequent turnover, and many of them, quite young. Nor need we wince at the thought of a training period brief enough to fit in with the short tenure. We should be unworried at the thought of modest salaries also commensurate with the brief training and tenure. Here we visualize something after the fashion of the Peace Corps, into which, for a short time, we channel the energy and enthusiasm of a large number of young workers not interested in teaching as a lifetime career. Young women, particularly, might appreciate a job in which moderate training and a short period of tenure would be the expectation.

For such a group of young teachers, of course, considerable guidance would seem wise. And at this point we encounter professionalization in the real sense. For every so many basic teachers there must be a responsible experienced teacher to act as a leader, or as an example, as in the current pattern of team teaching. Team teaching, it will be remembered (Chapter 7), results in no loss of efficiency, even though it may not be the panacea often contemplated. These experienced teachers, looking forward to teaching as a career, must have much more in the way of professional training. Since they constitute only a small fraction of the total staff, moreover, it should be possible to allot them quite generous salaries.

Such an arrangement may well result in an imbalance of the sexes. A brief career could be expected to have more appeal to young women than to young men. If the men going into teaching were largely interested in teaching as a life work, we would find a disproportionate number of men among the experienced, career teachers, and a preponderance of women among the younger basic teachers.

Along with the young, transient, basic teachers, and along with the professional career teachers, we clearly need the remedial specialist. As already mentioned, the need for this specialist seems inescapable. In any system, no matter how ambitious, no matter how elaborate the program for selecting teachers, and no matter how expensive and prolonged the program of training, there are bound to be children who fail to make an adequate response to the procedures available. Under the easygoing approach here contemplated, this inevitable fact is accepted, and it is proposed that these exceptions be treated as they arise.

We envisage, then, a third level of professionalization. This level consists of the remedial specialist who is called in when any child fails to respond to the treatment provided by the basic teacher under the direction of a career teacher. Such a specialist has at his disposal a great deal of knowledge. He is skilled in the more elaborate techniques of diagnosis. He can provide or direct remedial treatment. The members of this group must be highly trained and carefully selected. Obviously, they must be well paid.

In suggesting this hierarchy of professionalization, we are clearly influenced by the familiar pattern of caring for the physical well-being of the child. The general methods employed in the physical care of the child seem much more sensible and economical than any probable alternative. To insist that every mother should be a qualified pediatrician or an expert in nutrition seems ridiculous in the extreme. It seems much better to use the simple, unworrisome, routine procedures as far as they will go and to call on the specialist when things do not go well.

In the educational world it seems similarly unwise to insist that each classroom teacher be able to manage all exceptional problems on his own. The classroom teacher will have only occasional need for this skill. Secondly, the necessary skill is hard to obtain and would be ridiculously expensive to secure in every teacher. Finally, it is extremely questionable if the orientation and approach of the specialist is a desirable orientation for the regular classroom teacher. The remedial specialist, after all, is bound to be oriented toward pathology and the abnormal. He must be "problem-minded." But it may be unwise for the classroom teacher to be oriented to pedagogical pathology, just as it may be unwise for the average mother to have a doctor's book open before her at all times. It may be better for both teacher and mother to assume that, for the most part, things will go along fairly smoothly. For them the emphasis should be on the ruggedness of children and on their powers to adapt themselves to almost any reasonable regimen. Any attempt to convert all regular teachers into amateur psychopathologists might get in the way of this ideal (Symonds, 1949).

If this hierarchy of professionalization should ever come to be the pattern, by the way, it might do something to alter the lowly prestige so frequently accorded the whole teaching profession (Chaper 8). For the transient basic teachers, of course, no great amount of professional prestige would be expected. For the expert remedial teacher, at the other extreme, there is a reasonable chance for considerable professional regard. The expert remedial teacher would have the advantages of (1) comparative rarity, (2) lengthy, detailed, and business-like training, and (3) high salary. Such an expert would also have a further advantage. In common with his much-envied remedial counterpart in the medical profession, he would come into the picture when there is a palpable emergency seeming to require expert attention. Here, we assume that it is fairly easy to acquire prestige and glamor if you deal with the exceptional, important, and conspicuous emergency, such as a broken leg. Prestige and glamor are not so likely to come if, like the typical mother, or the English "nanny," you spend your time in supervising a process which quietly and inconspicuously goes its own way, and which very often can be depended upon to manage itself.

Less Worry about Administration

In the spontaneous theory, the teacher is the central figure. The rest of the vast educational enterprise chiefly serves the purpose of permitting the teacher to give spontaneous expression to the educated man he finds within himself—and, in so doing, to foster useful intellectual growth in his pupils.

In this teacher-centric approach what place do we find for the administrator? First of all it is reasonable to expect the administrator to act as a symbol for educational values. If we demand that the teacher symbolize things of the mind, we might be even more insistent that the chief school officers do likewise. The school can better apply its important sanctions if its most conspicuous members clearly represent its values in an attractive manner. It is perhaps too much to demand that a conspicuous administrator should also be a scholar. But people should think of scholarship when he is around.

Clearly there are also practical things to do. There is the crucial matter of support, both moral and practical. Someone must be sure that the teacher receives the peculiar moral support necessary for his craft (Chapter 10). Someone must arrange for salaries and for the necessary physical facilities. In complex communities, someone must be sure that pupils and teachers associate with each other.

At times the administrator can also help the teacher or arrange that someone else help him in the actual management of the teaching process. This function, although acknowledged, is not stressed in the current account.

Whatever he may do about helping the teacher, the administrator must also act as judge. Someone must decide whom to appoint, whom to promote, whom to discharge. Our theory, of course, would urge the administrator to avoid any pretence of being precise in these matters. In making decisions about prospective or actual competence in teaching, he is working in hideous darkness. He must still make decisions, but he should avoid the illusion of omniscience.

There may be some doubt, by the way, that the role of helper and the role of judge can be effectively combined in the same person. The jobs of providing help, on the one hand, and of judging, promoting, discharging on the other, may be so antithetical that they ought to be carried on by two separate staffs. To profit most from a "helping" supervisor, the teacher in trouble should feel quite free to reveal his weaknesses and shortcomings. But this might not be the best way to get promoted, or even to keep one's job. Ideally, perhaps, the "helping" supervisors ought to be forthrightly chosen and engaged by the teachers, subject to the call of the teachers, and pledged not to reveal their observations to the administrator. The "judging" supervisors, on the other hand, would be frankly inquisitorial, and concerned with the grim business of making the necessary decisions. Their real responsibility would be to judge. Their urge to help, if indulged, should not interfere with their sterner duty.

Insofar as either the "helping" function or the "judging" function calls for classroom visitation, we would expect a further complication. According to the spontaneous theory, it would not be surprising if a teacher, dimly aware of the rather earthy mechanisms on which he relied, might be reluctant to expose those ordinary procedures to the administrative eye. There is even a danger that the spontaneous expression of his interests may be dampened by the presence of an important observer. In any case, we would expect many teachers to be less than enthusiastic about the practice of classroom visitation, especially when this is used for evaluation.

All in all, there is much to justify a more relaxed and confident attitude toward the schools. Even with modest provisions much acceptable growth is likely to occur. Through elaborate modifications brought on by frenzied and agonizing decisions we can hope, not to transform this moderate growth, but merely to augment it, and possibly to give it minor redirection, perhaps to better ends, perhaps to worse.

In a body of teachers, selected by fairly ordinary means, we could expect to find the specialized concerns and compulsions from which schooling basically stems. There must be some administrative agency to select and assign these teachers. The administrator can also do much to obtain the necessary support—physical and moral—for the teachers, and to make their lives more comfortable. But he is the servant of the earthy forces on which he relies, not their controller.

In any system, no matter how elaborate, we must expect the occasional academic deficiency, although, in a system carrying the aura of exceptional precision, the inevitability of such deficiency may be masked. In a system avowedly relying on haphazard and ordinary mechanisms, however, the expectation of occasional failure, although no more real, is brought home in more compelling fashion. Of all the deliberate modifications contemplated, the most important would be those needed for occasional remedial treatment.

REFERENCES

Symonds, P. M., Education and psychotherapy, *J. educ. Psychol.*, 1949, *40*, 1–32.

12 | ASSESSING THE THEORY: Hypotheses in Search of a Test

The statements presented so far, however assertive they may sound, must clearly be regarded as hypotheses. Some of these hypotheses are quite extreme. And, in any case, extreme or trite, it would be amazing if some of them did not turn out to be false. Having examined the nature and implications of these hypotheses, it is time to consider the problem of subjecting them to experimental tests.

We must not be too apologetic, by the way, for deferring until this last section the problem of testing the hypotheses. Bannister (1966), continuing earlier warnings, has humorously pointed out the dangers of starting too soon to focus attention on experimental tests. Although stressing the importance of experiment as a final test, he notes that preoccupation with experimental niceties in the early stages of thinking may prevent us from ever entertaining some important notions.

Testing the Theory: Some General Problems

Throughout the discussion we have insisted that the school will continue to produce its modest results, and will obstinately ignore the administrative or organizational niceties that may be imposed. We have supported this contention with a vast array of experiments which regularly report no significant differences whenever administrative factors are manipulated. And now we propose a new series of experiments to test the theory itself! How can we escape this seeming inconsistency in which, in one breath, we suggest that experimental tests are bound to fail, and, in the next, we suggest additional experiments?

But there is no real inconsistency. The main argument by no means maintains that there are no forces which will affect educational achievement. On the contrary, it professes to specify those forces. It is in championing these basic, earthy forces that the theory notes the ineffectiveness of the deliberate, rational changes that are imposed upon them. Similarly, the long record of experimental failure is produced, not to show that no experiment can hope to display results but to show that experiments are likely to fail so long as they concentrate on the administrative features of schooling. If experiments turn to the genuine psychological forces that actually produce schooling, who knows what results may appear?

In this argument, we may also invoke the analogy of physical growth. In this area one could properly point to many experiments in which one gross, complex diet appeared to be as good as another gross, complex diet. One could also postulate a theory claiming that the essential dietary forces reside not in the gross diet as a whole, but in small, pervasive entities likely to be found in a great many diets. In spite of the ubiquitous nature of these entities in food as it is ordinarily eaten, one could propose experiments designed to detect the influence of these more lowly entities. In expecting, and in observing, failures of experiments with these gross diets, we are not automatically led to expect failure in experiments which deal with the basic forces at work within any diet.

In one practical respect, it is true, we may be foredoomed to an exercise in futility. If the postulated forces are present at optimal strength in almost any regimen, then no matter what we come to know about them, there is little useful contribution that we can make. If any conceivable diet is likely to contain an abundance of phosphorus, for instance, then from an immediate practical view, there is little to be gained from knowing the role of phosphorous in nutrition.

In the position taken here, such immediate practical considerations will play little part. In the first place we simply cannot tell how more precise knowledge of the basic forces may contribute to practice. And, in the second place, we must honor the sheer need to understand. Ignorance of an intriguing, pervasive process is an affront to the intellect and is not to be endured.

The Claims of Plausibility   Plausibility is often reluctantly invoked as a substitute for an experimental test. When such a test is out of the question, for either theoretical or practical reasons, an appeal to plausibility may be all that is left. And at many points we shamelessly rely on undocumented plausibility.

Even when an experimental test is contemplated, however, plausibility is still a matter for some concern. Ordinarily, hypotheses must have some appearance of plausibility before we will go to the trouble of considering a test. Few people would ever read about a proposed test, let alone undertake it, if the hypotheses involved were completely outrageous and had no suggestion of plausibility.

Are the current hypotheses plausible enough to justify the consideration of a test? Is it reasonable to expect, for instance, that the school by relying, only on the spontaneous expression of its scholastic interest, and making little or no use of a program of instruction, could develop a substantial amount of educational growth?

In considering the plausibility of this claim, one is inevitably impressed by the analogy of the home, and by the amount of learning and development which takes place in that institution. Unaided by anything in the way of formal instruction, for instance, and based almost entirely on the spontaneous forces of education within the home, the child learns a new language, and in that language he ordinarily acquires a good deal of proficiency. He develops habits of dressing, eating, and sleeping that largely conform to the pressure of the community. He acquires a complex structure of attitudes, fears, opinions, and hesitations. He learns subtle ways of reacting to other people. Altogether the sheer amount of learning acquired in this way challenges, if it does not surpass, the amount of learning induced by the schools.

Obviously, however, it would be unwise to push this analogy too far. Like most analogies, the resemblance between the home and the school is to be used merely to elucidate. It is not put forward as proof. And the resemblance may be incomplete. According to our own sociological speculations, after all, the home deals with vital affairs. For the development of these matters nature cannot afford to take any chances. The school, in contrast, deals with more deferrable activities, and there is less evolutionary insistence that these areas be developed by dependable, earthy forces. Consequently it is distinctly possible that the mechanisms actually at work in the schools are not those earthy forces on which the home depends. We can merely claim that since such spontaneous forces do work in the home, there is no a priori reason why they could not work within the school.

To point to the possibility of substantial psychological development apart from the influence of deliberate instruction, we can also invoke the child's increased mastery of the material in the typical intelligence tests. These tests are designed to measure achievement in matters which receive little, if any, emphasis in the school. Ordinarily these tests make a point of avoiding items which are encountered only in the formalized program of the school. Such tests give chief emphasis to items encountered in casual, every-day experience. Items in intelligence tests refer to the meanings of ordinary words, and not to the meaning of technical words. They present problems in ordinary arithmetic and avoid problems which call for highly technical processes.

To acquire any mastery whatever over the materials in an intelligence test, we must depend upon the haphazard impact of raw experience. Whatever growth there may be, it must come from the unguided, undeliberate, spontaneous reactions of the learner, and from the equally spontaneous and undirected actions of those around him.

The growth that comes from this haphazard impact of raw experience is very substantial indeed. As the years go by the child masters tasks of increasing complexity. He learns new words. He also learns harder words. As he becomes even more mature he can detect logical absurdities or discern subtle distinctions in ethics.

This evidence, with all its dependence on a questionable analogy, does provide some support for the plausibility of the spontaneous hypothesis. We might readily expect the simple, casual expression of the school's concern for Latin to induce development in that trait, just as the undirected action of the haphazard environment induces a mastery of the tasks in the typical intelligence test.

The Interaction between Spontaneous and Deliberate Forces   As one of its crucial assumptions, the theory insists that we can distinguish between spontaneous forces and deliberate forces. Part of the theory is concerned with the way in which these two sets of forces interact with each other or supplement each other. As yet the theory has failed to say whether this distinction is qualitative or quantitative—whether it is in the nature of a dichotomy or a dimension. It does assume, however, that some useful distinction can be made.

I am indebted to Professor John Walton, by the way, for the suggestion that other social sciences could profit from an emphasis on spontaneous versus deliberate forces, and on the ways in which they interact. In law, in government, and in marriage customs it may be useful to see how far the unthinking, spontaneous pressures will carry matters, and at what point, and in what way, deliberate rational pressures are exerted.

Conditions Favorable to a Test

As suggested in the analogy of physical growth, there are some practical difficulties to be dealt with if we are to test a theory such as that proposed. We are dealing with a process that has tremendous practical consequences. Light-hearted meddling in this vital process, for scientific or other reasons, is not to be tolerated. In many cultures we are also dealing with forces that are already present in some profusion, and this may complicate things. Important dietary experiments may be much easier to manage where there is now a dietary deficit than where the postulated ingredients are overbundant. Similarly, in schooling, adequate investigations could best be carried out in an area in which there are now minimal facilities.

A Retreat to the Ivory Tower To test hypotheses as radical and as potentially dangerous as those contemplated, one might well seek to guard against any premature application to the practical world of the schools. For this reason, investigations carried on within some ivory tower might have much to recommend them. This is not to deny, of course, that, ultimately, theory and practice are mutually interdependent. Practice, undoubtedly, should be based on sound theory when such is available. Theory, in turn, must look to practice for initial data, for fruitful hypotheses, and for final tests. It would be ridiculous to suggest that either of these activities could, or should, function for any length of time completely out of contact with the other.

But it is one thing to make provision for frequent contact, or ready access, and quite another thing to insist on a complete and continuous merging of two activities. There is much to recommend the establishment of separate zones of privacy for both theory and practice. Each could then retire into its own zone for a time and forget about the concerns of the other.

Such a temporary separation certainly has much to offer the practical administrator. Although obligated to keep in touch with *tested* ideas and with theories that have survived intensive and critical scrutiny, he should feel no obligation to keep in touch with every tentative and untried suggestion that arises in the fertile brain of some theorist. The lifting of that improper obligation should give the administrator enormous peace of mind with respect to the constant flow of suggestions which now keep the educational scene in continual turmoil. Only a limited number of ideas per decade will survive the rigorous testing to which all ideas should be subjected, and with only this limited number to bother about, the administrator would be free to go ahead and keep the school system running.

The occasional and temporary separation of theory from practice should also have great advantages for the theorist. Having saturated himself in the existing data and in the problems that face the practitioner, the theorist could then retire into his zone of privacy. Within these walls he need feel no restriction. He should be free to indulge the wildest flights of fancy and to concoct the most bizarre and radical theoretical structures. He knows that none of his fantastic conceptions will be forced upon the general public, and his products carry the clear label of "experimental and subject to test."

Such activity is greatly needed in the field of educational theory. We could profit from new and radical hypotheses or explanations which have no concern for the probable consequences but which look only for an adequate understanding and description of the facts. Such bold and rigorous theorizing, carried on within the lodge, may ultimately lead to revolutionary concepts which, if they survive the necessary testing and scrutiny, may be offered to the public with vast gains to practice.

Developing an Attitude Favorable to Avowed Experimentation   It has been suggested that theories should receive careful, rigorous tests before being widely incorporated into educational practice. Until recently, however, it has been difficult to secure permission and support for experiments that carry the necessary controls. True enough we welcome widespread innovations. Let all the children in a school system be subjected to an untried procedure, and we applaud in the name of progress. Let a few volunteers try out the same procedure in a cautious preliminary test, and we talk about guinea pigs and callous experimentation. If this paradoxical emotional attitude can be modified, it should be quite possible to initiate the changes in such graduated doses that no child will suffer any disadvantage that could not be speedily corrected.

The Need for Large Numbers of Classrooms   In many of the investigations here proposed, the teacher is the basic unit. This means there is the need for a large number of classrooms in which the teachers could function. Often it will be necessary that some of the differences between classes be balanced out or brought under control. This may be done by random assignment or by careful counterbalancing. In either case large numbers are essential.

Utilizing Educational Expansion   When any educational facility is first being introduced, it is the time to test its worth. After the new treatment has become the mode, we will find it difficult to turn back the clock in an attempt to determine the worth of the innovation.

Fortunately, as it happens, many current innovations (e.g. head start) are being introduced in an experimental situation in which a comparable control group is employed. The current prudence about the use of control groups, however, does not help in the evaluation of facilities long established.

To determine the influence of many facilities, now taken for granted in Western culture, it would be natural to carry on investigations in regions where education is rapidly expanding. Typically such experimentation could be carried on with no danger of exploiting the people involved. Suppose, for instance, we contemplate increasing the period of training for teachers. Ordinarily, at the outset, there are not enough facilities to provide additional training for everybody. With a little foresight the new treatment could be given to selected people in such a way that the worth of the treatment could be determined.

Hypotheses to Be Tested

Some of the hypotheses to be discussed deal with the general background notions put forward in the tentative speculative portion of our theory. These are dealt with briefly. The data necessary for testing these hypotheses, as a matter of fact, may already be in the possession of those more familiar with the fields of sociology and anthropology. The more psychological hypotheses, on the other hand, are discussed in more detail.

Background Hypotheses The general sociological speculations, when refined and purged of tautologies, will have to be tested by an appeal to historical and anthropological data. From such data we could see if schools or near schools are almost universal. We could see, too, if such schools did, as claimed, give chief emphasis to those areas for which the members of the more immediate family felt a remote and indulgent concern.

It is in regions in which formal schools are just being established that we might find it easiest to test the claim that the emphasis given by the school reflects, inversely, the urgency of parental concern. Here it might be possible to rate parental preoccupations with respect to urgency. Parents could also indicate the things that the schools should teach. Prospective, but untrained, teachers from the same community could also be asked about an appropriate curriculum for the schools. Trained teachers, of course, would be less useful since they would probably merely vote for the subjects they had been taught.

A second background hypothesis (Chapter 5) deals with the relation of the school's influence to that of the nonscholastic factors such as maturation, home influence, and the general influence of the community. Some aspects of this hypothesis have already been tested by analyses such as those of Kemp (1955), Wiseman (1964), and Greenfield (1964). Using either regression analysis or a factorial design, these studies have examined the variance to be found in academic achievement and have attempted to determine how much of that variance can be attributed to various background factors and how much can be linked with scholastic variables such as school size, class size, teacher morale, teacher training and the like. So far the relations with the nonscholastic variables are more pronounced. We need more studies, however, in which the variations in scholastic provisions cover a wider range. We need to include communities, for instance, in which schooling is at a minimal level. We should also try to measure some of the attributes of schooling stressed in this theory, such as the interests and the communicative compulsions of the teachers.

As one of the background factors, the theory stresses the role of academic sanctions in furthering educational development. Apart from the Entwisle study (1961) mentioned in Chapter 5, this potential factor has received little attention. To examine the influence of sanctions and of the related Hawthorne effect, we should include, in our tests of any educational device, an additional group which receives all the trappings of the device but not the actual content transmitted by the device. In an investigation of the value of "head-start" programs, for instance, we need groups who go through all the motions of head start but who do not receive the additional training supplied by head start. Such control groups would have to be given pseudotraining instead. They would receive talk *about* the importance of early training. They would participate in training sessions but would be exposed to language incomprehensible to them (or perhaps to anyone). Visual materials would be presented too rapidly to be seen. The children in this group should feel that competence in these areas is considered important, and some significant people expect them to do well in such areas. The gains of this group would indicate the power of sanctions plus the Hawthorne factor to induce growth, even in the absence of overt instruction.

The hypotheses just described deal in rather general fashion with the sociological setting in which the school functions. They deal with the broad background factors which must be kept in mind if we are to understand the more specific forces that operate within the school itself.

In contrast to these background hypotheses, the more specific hypotheses about to be discussed deal with the conduct of teachers and the actual operation of the school.

Overt Statements of Objectives   In many prevailing views of schooling, a clear-cut formulation of objectives is considered essential to success (Chapter 6). As its very first concern, the typical evaluating committee asks whether or not the school in question has any clear idea of what it hopes to accomplish. Without such a grasp of objectives, how could it be expected to accomplish anything?

In contrast to the prevailing view, the theory of spontaneous schooling would attach little importance to the formal statement of objectives. When powerful primitive urges are at work we can often disregard the overt protestations of objectives. The actual conduct of the lover, for instance, can be predicted more accurately from a knowledge of his urges than from any logical analysis he may give us to account for his interest in his beloved.

The claims of the spontaneous theory, in this respect, could be tested by a two-way factorial design. As one of the independent variables, we would need a number of schools differing widely in the philosophic position espoused or in the educational goals professed. We have in mind differences that might arise regarding concern for creativity as opposed to concern for the mastery of the traditional, or emphasis on education for real life as opposed to education for academic mastery. As our second independent variable we need assessments of the lively, spontaneous interests of teachers within the various schools. We need sufficient teachers to permit an orthogonal design in which the whole range of lively interests would be present in each of the schools with differing rationales. Two dependent variables should be used. One of these consists of descriptions of classroom activities, the descriptions or classifications being made in ignorance of the prevailing philosophy. The second is the actual achievement of the pupils in areas encompassed by the differing philosophies.

It would be necessary to use covariance or other devices to control such background factors as maturation, intelligence, home pressures, and community pressures. Ideally we should also have groups exposed to pseudoinstruction to provide a control for general sanctions and for the Hawthorne effect.

Our theory would predict a significant effect, in both dependent variables, from the lively interests of the teachers, formal curriculum being balanced out. The theory would also predict only a slight or insignificant effect from curriculums when teacher interests are balanced out.

In predicting a lack of relation between professed purpose on the one hand and classroom activities on the other, the hypothesis also invites an historical test. In the past, schools have operated under a large number of philosophic rationales. They have taken on the tasks, for instance, of bringing man closer to God, of exorcizing some of the demons that prevailed within the child, of making him a better citizen, of disciplining his mind, of achieving an on-going expansion of his essential inner self. According to our spontaneous theory, an examination of the classroom activities of these different schools would reveal a marked similarity.

As warrants, not for the truth of this hypothesis but for its plausibility, we might consider widespread concern about the discrepancy between the espoused curriculum on the one hand and the teacher-produced *de facto* curriculum on the other. D. H. Morrel (Various, 1963), for instance, wonders whether or not we can justify the conduct of a teacher who is thus determining the curriculum. For other writers, the discrepancy between formal curriculum and teacher performance is clearly something to be deplored. Oliver (1953) has noted the uncooperative behavior of teachers in this matter. A decade later Wallen and Travers (1963, p. 463) lament the same intransigeance. Teachers just cannot be depended upon to make their classroom behavior conform to the bright new policies derived from even the most compelling rationale.

In the view advanced here, there is no serious place for deploring or exulting. From our hypothesis, as a matter of fact, we would expect some benefits from the power of the postulated forces to go their own way somewhat indifferent to the tortured decisions that beat out each new change in policy. Although this independence would nullify the good to be gained from the great and true rationale, it would, by the same token, guarantee a great deal of academic development even when the directors of schooling have only a nebulous notion of what the schools should do, or even when they have a perverted notion of the school's appropriate function.

Along with the principal predictions of this hypothesis, we must note a number of qualifications. We would expect, for instance, a number of interactions. The first of these is the simple statistical interaction between the two independent variables (formal statement of objectives and lively interests of teachers). This is illustrated in the following table.

Hypothetical Statement of Academic Gains in Relation to Overt Curricular Stress and to Lively Teacher Interest

	Student Gains in Creativity		
Curricular Stress on Creativity	*Interest of Teachers in Creativity*		
	Lacking or Moderate	Vivid	Average
High	4.0	7.0	5.5
Low or Absent	1.0	6.0	3.5
Average	2.5	6.5	4.5

In the table we restate our expectation of a marked difference for teacher interests but a minor, perhaps insignificant, difference for curricular emphasis. We also indicate, however, that teacher interest will be most effective when the curricular stress is low, and, conversely, there may well be some influence of curricular stress when teacher interest is lacking or moderate.

In the contemplated *ex post facto* investigation, there is a second kind of interaction which we must take into account. Here we visualize two or more schools, only one stressing creativity. But in both schools we must be able to find some teachers having a burning concern for creativity and others lacking this urge. In schools already staffed, however, we might expect to find a correlation between the professed concern of the school and the actual urge of the teacher. If we are able to fill all the cells of our table, we might have to search hard for "noncreative" teachers in the "creative" schools or for "creative" teachers in the "noncreative" schools. These hard-to-find teachers, moreover, are exceptions by definition. They might also be well aware of their nonconformist status, and this awareness, in turn, might well affect their teaching.

A further type of interaction might appear in any long-term study of curricular innovations. Within our theory there are indirect avenues through which a formal curricular decision could bring about important results. In announcing a decision, for instance, that Russian is now to be taught, the school board would call attention to the importance of Russian in the educational scheme of things and would thus extend the general educational sanctions to this subject. If this convinces people that Russian is now an attribute of the educated man, many educational forces will automatically be set in motion (Chapter 5). Such a statement could also attract into the profession people who are already interested in Russian but who had not thus far thought of teaching. The statement could also bring out latent interests in the subject on the part of a few teachers now in the profession.

The School's Success in Different Tasks   The theory has had much to say (Chapter 9) about the probable success of the school as it addresses itself first to one task and then to another. The natural curriculum (Chapters 3 and 4) is held to lie in that region of activities for which parents and society in general have a long-range, sporadic, indulgent concern, but for which they feel little immediate, vivid, day-by-day involvement. Intense, moment-by-moment concern on the part of other agencies would render the curriculum superfluous. Complete lack of interest would deprive that curriculum of its necessary support. Consider, first, the claim that pronounced and continuous parental interest would reduce the net affect of the school's efforts. To test this claim we could readily use children from the so-called middle classes who now value the traditional academic curriculum of the school. Thinking of these middle-class children, our hypothesis holds that the school will have more net success in teaching such academic subjects as algebra or Latin than in teaching the pervasive virtues of cooperation, social grace, or good citizenship.

In all this, it is the net influence of the school that we have in mind. To determine the net influence of the school (as opposed to its gross influence) in teaching ballroom dancing, for instance, we would need two groups of children, all mature enough to participate in ballroom dancing. These two groups should be comparable in everything which might affect growth in dancing. They should also have about the same mastery of dancing at the beginning of the experiment. When these matters have been arranged, one of the groups will be given instruction by the school and the other will not. At the end of the year or at some other period of time, the status of each group will again be determined and the growth of each group ascertained. The net influence of the school will be the difference between the growth of the "taught" and the growth of the "untaught" group. If, for instance, the group subjected to schooling gained forty points on the dancing test, and the untaught group gained ten points, the net influence of the school would be thirty points.

For many reasons it will be convenient to express the net influence of the school as a fraction of the total growth. Rather than saying that the net influence of the school is thirty points on an arbitrary scale, we would do better to say that this net influence is thirty-fortieths or three-fourths of the total growth or to say that three-fourths of the total growth observed in the instructed group could be attributed to the influence of the school. Such a fraction is more immediately intelligible and requires relatively little interpretation. It also gets rid of the arbitrary nature of each scale or measuring instrument and thus makes possible a comparison from one kind of measurement, say, speed of swimming, to another, say, knowledge of Tennyson.

The fraction used to indicate the net influence of the school can range from one to zero or even to a negative fraction. If the untaught group gains nothing whatever, the fraction would be

$$\frac{\text{Gain of Taught} - 0}{\text{Gain of Taught}} \text{ or Unity}$$

If the gains of the two groups were identical, the numerator, and hence the fraction, would be zero. If, by some chance, the untaught group should gain more than the taught group, the fraction would be negative, showing that the school actually interfered with growth in this trait.

This fraction would act as a very general index of the net influence of the school. For more precise purposes, it would have to be refined, and certain corrections would have to be considered. There is the whole problem, for instance, of the equality of units on the different portions of the scale. But for general purposes it would give a fair indication of the school's effectiveness.

According to the hypothesis to be tested, the net influence of the school should rise as we move from subjects, such as honesty, for which there is pronounced parental and community concern to subjects such as algebra for which the concern is merely indulgent and supportive. As we approach other subjects for which there is no parental support whatever, we would expect the net influence of the school to decline.

With the middle-class children so far envisaged, it might be difficult to detect the expected decline as we approach the more rarefied academic subjects. No matter how recondite the subject to be introduced, its very introduction into the school's curriculum may induce its own indulgent support. For classes living in this tradition, there may be some support for anything the school may choose to do.

To test the notion that the school will be most effective when there is at least moderate parental support, we might find it more convenient to use children from the so-called underprivileged groups. For such groups the curriculum of the traditional school may well represent the region of zero parental or group interest. If such is the case, our theory would predict that the school would have more net influence if it adopted a curriculum which reflected the marginal, but substantial, interests of adults in this group. It should reflect the things the adults would like to see accomplished but which they fail to care for. For some groups, a curriculum emphasizing folk music, athletics, and social one-upmanship might show more net returns than one stressing topics for which there is little or no residual adult concern.

To predict that a given curriculum might be more effective or might show more net returns, is not the same thing as recommending such a curriculum. This curriculum might be more effective but in the wrong direction or in a useless direction. And if the development of academic skill is a social must for the underprivileged groups, we should perhaps impose that curriculum in spite of the heavy going it is likely to encounter.

For the long-range effect, we might suggest, in passing, there might be some advantage in teaching the "effective" things at first. Then, when the schools were accepted as a useful institution by the groups in question, we might gradually alter the *de facto* curriculum—by changes in staff or otherwise—toward more desirable goals. But these offhand suggestions are not to be confused with hypotheses put forward for serious testing.

The Effect of the Postulated Tendencies   A complete test of each of the postulated tendencies would call for a rather complex factorial design. We should have teachers varying in knowledge of a given subject, in interest in the subject, in tendency to talk about the subject by commenting on statements other people make about the subject, by supplying the answer, and by pointing the moral. As a preliminary test, however, we might combine knowledge and interest into one dimension and also collapse the various communicative compulsions into a single dimension. We should examine the effect of these factors when sense of mission (overt intention to teach) is at a minimum and also when the mission is more pronounced. This suggests a three-by-three-by-two design, having three gradations of knowledge-interest, three of communicativeness, and two degrees of mission.

The zero-mission or minimum-mission state may be difficult to obtain. In developing the theory (Chapter 6), we suggested asking people to supervise a classroom that had been left unscheduled for an hour per day. Other less formal situations may be available. Adults in charge of dining tables in a boarding school might provide the necessary association and yet not feel obliged to teach. In a camping situation, adults might be made responsible for the physical welfare of children and for sustained contact and yet be given no formal responsibility to instruct.

Introducing a sense of mission, would present no practical problems. Certain people could be asked to give instruction in the subject in question. Care would have to be taken to be sure that the "missionless" teachers did not learn of this assignment, but this could be managed in various ways.

There should be little problem in obtaining measures of the "teachers'" knowledge of various subjects or of interest in them. The assessment of communicative tendencies, however, is a difficult matter. In a number of pilot studies in the Canadian Armed Forces, we have tried "buddy" ratings. Devices were developed which gave satisfactory consistency when the ratings of one random half of a platoon were correlated with the other half.

Our preliminary trials did not permit us to examine the validity of these devices, although, at one stage, we had indirect evidence of lack of validity. To our Canadian troops, our early descriptions of communicativeness (talking a lot about———) suggested "the guy who is always shooting off his mouth," and we got highly reliable indices of the platoon rejects! Later phrasings were able to eliminate this connotation.

Presumably the ratings for communicativeness could be checked against direct observation of the people in a relatively free situation. If these laborious approaches did suggest validity, the more simple rating device could be used for the main populations.

Social Impact of the Teacher The effective teacher is one who, among other things, spontaneously emits approval or disapproval. If this kind of reinforcement is to be effective, however, the teacher must be the kind of person whose approval or disapproval matters. To measure this trait of social impact, we might use simple ratings by students who had been exposed to the teacher. Students might be asked to indicate those teachers whose approval (and/or disapproval) meant a great deal to them. The number of students nominating any teacher in either category would thus be an index of the teacher's impact. As an additional or alternative method of measuring this trait, one might use an objective performance record. Under such a procedure, for instance, students might be given a favorable report card. They would then be told that the report card had to be countersigned by some teacher, but as far as possible they could take the report to any teacher they wished. The students would then list the teachers in order of preference, with a view to arranging a suitable schedule. At a different time the students would receive an unfavorable report card with the same instructions. A teacher's social impact would be indicated by the number of children who placed that teacher high on the list when they had a favorable report card and by the number of children who placed him low on the list when they had an unfavorable report.

Spontaneous Forces versus Administrative Refinements The basic forces reside in the primitive concerns and tendencies to be found in teachers. Compared to the growth induced by these forces, the effect of administrative devices is considered to be minor.

We could test this claim by incorporating some kind of an administrative dimension into the three-by-three-by-two design intended to test the effect of the postulated spontaneous tendencies. Such an extended design would then consist of three degrees of knowledge-interest, three degrees of communicativeness, two degrees of mission, and n degrees of administrative provisions.

It is ridiculous to assume that there really is a single dimension of administrative provisions. Theoretically each kind of administrative device should be scaled separately and incorporated into our design as a separate factor. If we are to examine any number of such devices, however, we would have a grotesquely complex design. To avoid such an unwieldy design, we might compromise by having school systems rated along a dimension that ranged from a primitive-impoverished administration, at one extreme, to a sophisticated-lavish administration, at the other. The impoverished extreme would be represented by the primitive model suggested in Chapter 11. In this model, it will be remembered, we merely had arranged that a group of "teachers" be selected in a very gross fashion, and they be induced to associate with children. Departures from this primitive base line might be rated with enough precision to justify three or four categories of administrative lavishness.

In thus lumping together a large number of different administrative devices, we clearly run risks. Some specific devices if tested by themselves might help. Others might hurt. An unanalyzed combination might show no effect.

From such a design two kinds of expectations would be in order. The first has to do with the main effects and represents an intrinsic test of the theory. Our theory, obviously, would predict that the main effects attributable to the administrative dimension would be markedly less than the effects attributable to knowledge-interest, to communicative tendencies, or to mission. The second expectation deals with interactions and refers not to the truth or falsity of the theory but to the impact of the spontaneous forces on other variables. From the interactions, for instance, we should get some information about the effect of sequence as discussed in Chapter 7. If it is true that we can expect more results from early applications of any force than from later applications, this fact should show up in the interactions. We should find, in the first place, a significant interaction effect. The trend of these interactions should also show that any one dimension had a more pronounced effect when it was applied at a low stage of the other dimensions. Some administrative influence should be revealed, for instance, when mission and the spontaneous factors were at a moderate level. This influence should fall off markedly, however, when the more basic forces were present in some strength.

This sketch of possible tests, for all its descent into technical jargon, is in no sense a detailed blueprint. To some extent, this lack of detail may come from sheer inertia and from a very ignoble reluctance to work out the necessary steps. As so often happens, however, such a primitive reluctance may contain an unexpected justification. Just as it may be unwise to be too precipitous in worrying about any kind of experimentation in the early stages of theory development, so it may also be unwise to be too forward in spelling out the specific details when we do approach the grim tasks of an experimental test. The broad pattern of testing may be specified in advance. But the details of any one test will stem more from the preceding tests than from the broad conditions envisaged at the outset.

REFERENCES

Bannister, D., Psychology as an exercise in paradox, *Bull. Brit. Psychol. Soc.*, 1966, *19*, No. 63, 21–26.

Entwisle, Doris R., Attensity: factors of specific set in school learning, *Harv. educ. Rev.*, 1961, *31*, 84–101.

Greenfield, B. T., Administration and systems analysis, *Canad. Administrator*, 1964, *3*, (No. 7), 25–30.

Kemp, L. C. D., Environmental and other characteristics determining attainment in primary schools, *Brit. J. educ. Psychol.*, 1955, *25*, 67–77.

Oliver, W. A., Teachers' educational beliefs versus their classroom practices, *J. educ. Res.*, 1953, *47*, 47–55.

Various, Curriculum study and the freedom of the teacher, *Educ. Res.*, 1963, *5*, 83–103.

Wallen, N. E., and R. M. W. Travers, Analysis and investigation of teaching methods, in N. L. Gage, ed., *Handbook of research on teaching*. Skokie, Ill.: Rand McNally, 1963.

Wiseman, S., *Education and environment*. Manchester, England: University of Manchester Press, 1964.

INDEX

page numbers in *italics* indicate complete
bibliographical reference for an author

Curriculum construction, degree of precision, 133-134

DeCecco, J., 10, *15*, 75
Dedicated specialist, effective controls of, 125-127
support needed, 123-124
Deferred practice, limitations of, 54-55
Deliberate decisions, and curriculum construction, 43, 133-134
and evolution of schools, 34
indirect effects, 153
tasks of school, 45-46
Deliberate instruction, growth in absence of, 145-146
Deliberate intention, lack of, in teaching, 58
and spontaneous forces, interaction, 146
of teacher, and achievement, 76-77
in theories of teaching, 57
Deliberate versus spontaneous behavior, 34-35
in observed tendencies, 38-39
in teaching, 58
Delinquency prevention, effect of school, 111, 118
Dell, G. A., 111, *119*
Dessart, D. J., 81, *86*
Dessel, N. F., 55, *56*
Diminishing returns, and negative results, 84-85
Disadvantaged communities, effective curriculum, 155-156
Disapproval, spontaneous, 36-37
Discussion versus lecture, 10, 81
Disinterested study, of schooling, 5, 11, 19, 147-148
Domas, S. J., 94, *102*
Double classes, and achievement, 78-79
Douglass, H. R., 78, *87*
Dowling, F. R., 100, *102*
Downing, U. M., *88*
Dubos, R. J., 115, 117, *119*
Dysinger, D. W., 74, *87*

Eash, M. J., 75, *87*
Eaton, M. T., 73, *87*, *90*
Education, versus schooling, 20
Educational experiments, public attitude toward, 148
during expansion, 148-149
Educational psychology, in teacher training, 14
Effectance, and manipulative behavior, 28
Eight-year study, 81
Eisner, E. W., 57, *69*
Ekstrom, R., 10, *15*, 80
Elaborateness, and tasks of school, 33
Elementary ideas, emphasis in teaching, 95-96
Ellena, W. J., 94, *102*
Ellis, J. R., 73, *87*
Employment of students, and achievement, 78

Entwisle, D. R., 52, 53, 76, *87*, 150, *159*
Esoteric concerns, support and restraint, 122-123, 128-130
Esthetic imperative, in teacher training, 14
Eurich, A. C., 80, *88*
Examinations, frequency of, and achievement, 82
Experimenting, test of theory, 144-145
Explanations, nature of, 21, 22
Ex post facto studies, problems in, 153
Extended family, and schools, 7, 25
Extracurricular activities, and achievement, 78
Extraschool agencies, for real-life curriculum, 115

Factorial design, experiments on objectives, 151
spontaneous versus administrative factors, 157-158
Feldhusen, J. F., 10, 82, *87*
Feldman, M. E., 82, *87*
Films, teaching of attitudes, 110-111
Finch, F. H., 73, *87*
Flavell, J. H., 54, *55*
Fleming, C. M., 10, *15*, 75
Foreign language, in elementary school, 55
Freedman, M., 111, *119*, *120*
Freudian stages, real-life curriculum, 106-107
Friesen, E. J., 55, *55*
Fullerton, B. J., 81, *88*
Furness, E. L., 100, *102*

Gage, N. L., 3, *15*
Galanter, E., 61, *69*
Gardner, J. W., *131*
Garrett, H. F., 78, *87*
Gerberich, J. R., 80, *87*
Giffin, K., 75, *87*
Ginther, J. R., 10, *15*, 80
Goals, disagreement, real-life curriculum, 109
Goertzen, S. M., 117, *119*
Grade placement of subjects, 55
Grate, J. H., *88*
Gray, W. S., 80, *87*
Greene, E. B., 76, *87*
Greenfield, B. T., 149, *159*
Gropper, G. L., 77, *87*
Group-centered teaching, and achievement, 10, 81-82
Guidance (in learning), 61
and effective teaching, 97
spontaneous nature of, 65
Gump, P. V., 79, *86*
Guthrie, E. R., 61, *69*

Hall, C. V., 49, *53*
Hamblin, J. W., *90*
Harding, L. W., 80, *87*
Harlow, H. F., 28, *41*